THE
RETURNED
MISSIONARY
>> HANDBOOK <<

MARIANNA & STEVE RICHARDSON

THE
RETURNED
MISSIONARY
▸▸ HANDBOOK ◂◂

HELPING MISSIONARIES & PARENTS THROUGH THE POST-MISSION TRANSITION

CFI
An Imprint of Cedar Fort, Inc.
Springville, Utah

This is not an official publication of The Church of Jesus Christ of Latter-day Saints. The opinions and views expressed herein belong solely to the author and do not necessarily represent the opinions or views of Cedar Fort, Inc. Permission for the use of sources, graphics, and photos is also solely the responsibility of the author.

ISBN 13: 978-1-4621-1794-9

Published by CFI, an imprint of Cedar Fort, Inc.
2373 W. 700 S., Springville, UT 84663
Distributed by Cedar Fort, Inc., www.cedarfort.com

LIBRARY OF CONGRESS CATALOGING-IN-PUBLICATION DATA

Names: Richardson, Marianna Edwards, author. | Richardson, Steve, 1953- author.
Title: The returned missionary handbook : helping missionaries and parents through the post-mission transition / Marianna and Steve Richardson.
Description: Springville, Utah : CFI, an imprint of Cedar Fort, Inc., [2016] | ©2016 | Includes bibliographical references and index.
Identifiers: LCCN 2016007894 (print) | LCCN 2016009728 (ebook) | ISBN 9781462117949 (perfect bound : alk. paper) | ISBN 9781462126040 (epub, pdf, mobi)
Subjects: LCSH: Mormon missionaries. | Adjustment (Psychology)--Religious aspects--Christianity.
Classification: LCC BX8661 .R48 2016 (print) | LCC BX8661 (ebook) | DDC 222/.9332--dc23
LC record available at http://lccn.loc.gov/2016007894

Cover design by Shawnda T. Craig
Cover design © 2016 by Cedar Fort, Inc.
Edited and typeset by Rebecca Bird

Printed in the United States of America

10 9 8 7 6 5 4 3 2 1

Printed on acid-free paper

To our returned missionary children,
our returned missionaries from the Brazil São Paulo South Mission,
the returned missionaries we have taught,
and returned missionaries worldwide for generations to come—
We love you all!

Contents

Prologue for Returned Missionaries

Alyssa just finished her last email home to her parents. She couldn't believe how fast these eighteen months had flown by, especially the last few months. The last days of her mission felt like they were shorter than the usual twenty-four hours. She would miss so many investigators she'd been working with so diligently. She was sad that she wouldn't see many of their baptisms, but Julio had just decided to be baptized on her last Sunday in Chile. She couldn't wait!

Her parents were excited to see her, as well as her brothers and sisters. She was having a hard time thinking about it; she still had so much to do. Her mom kept pushing her to register for classes at BYU, but she didn't want to think about it right now. She figured that when she arrived home there would be plenty of time for those kinds of activities. Alyssa had a dark worry in the back of her mind that her life back home would not feel as important as her life felt on the mission. All her married sisters had more children while she'd been away. Some of her friends had married and were pregnant. Nobody was waiting for her at home and she didn't want to think about dating or boys anyway.

The day of her return finally came. There were tears, hugs, and good-byes, then more tears, hugs, and hellos as loving family and friends enveloped her. The rush of excitement reached a mighty crescendo as she gave her homecoming talk, and the glow of that moment stayed with her for days afterward.

Prologue for Returned Missionaries

After being home for a week, Alyssa continued to revel in the loving environment provided by her family, especially her new nieces and nephews. Her bed felt so wonderful every night, and she definitely did not miss Sister Hernandez's snoring. Yet, she felt an increasing emptiness as she wondered how her investigators were doing. Julio still had so many questions about the gospel! Alyssa was so thankful for Facebook and wrote daily to Julio and to her other dear investigators and new converts.

Her mother was still pressuring her to register for BYU and nudged her every time Nate Allen came into sight. He had just returned from his mission, too. She knew her mother was right about registering for BYU— she needed to do it, but she felt apathetic toward such worldly pursuits. And Nate! Well, it was just too weird to even think about socializing with a boy, let alone dating one. Her only concern right now was getting back on Facebook to see Julio's response to her comment on the importance of paying tithing.

You might be able to relate to Alyssa's feelings as she looked forward to coming home. You probably felt the same conflicting emotions of elation and excitement for family and friends, yet sadness and loss as you said goodbye to the people and the mission that you loved. Those conflicting emotions might still be churning inside of you. Now that you're home, you may be facing some of the same challenges Alyssa faced. You've changed and you don't know how to make those changes work with your old life. Do you return to the person you were before the mission, or do you continue being the person you became on the mission? If you continue as the person you've become, what will other people think? Will they think you're weird?

This book is designed to help you in your journey of spiritual self-discovery. Throughout the various chapters, you will find concepts that will help you focus on eternal principles, apply all the knowledge and skills that you acquired on your mission, and overcome the challenges you face. For those missionaries who have had to come home early for whatever reason, there is also a chapter written specifically for you—you may want to read that chapter first. The stories of missionaries in this book are taken from real experiences of returned missionaries, though the names have often been changed.

A brief overview of the chapters is as follows:

- **Coming Home.** Coming home is exciting, wonderful, and strange. After the initial excitement wears off, you may be left wondering, "Now what?"

- **Fulfilling Your Eternal Purpose.** Your purpose has not changed. Your focus on the gospel or doctrine of Christ should not be any different now that you are home. The eternal principles you taught your investigators, especially about the Atonement and its power in our lives, are still true. You must continue to hold on to the truth and put into practice these same principles.

- **Keeping the Glow!** When you first come home there is a discernible glow about you. Hold on to the light that emanates from within you by maintaining a spiritual oasis away from the world. You did this on your mission and you can continue to do it now.

- **Using *Preach My Gospel* Forever.** Continue to use *Preach My Gospel* as a resource throughout your life. Do not ignore this dear friend, which you read and studied from every day of your mission. You will be surprised by how relevant this inspired book still is.

- **Dealing with Family Changes.** Changes in your family can be dramatic while you have been on your mission—maybe your family moved to a new home, your mom had a baby, your brother got married without you, a grandparent passed away, or someone in your family left the church. A multitude of new and different situations are now a part of your life and you need to deal with them. Dealing with such changes can definitely be a trial when returning home.

- **Rising above Challenges.** You have already experienced and overcome many challenges while on your mission. Now, you must learn to rise above the new challenges you are facing in a positive, constructive, and spiritual way.

- **Coming Home Early.** No one leaves on a mission expecting to come home early. If you are a returned missionary in this situation, realize that other returned missionaries like you share your same feelings. Whether you came home early for emotional, physical, or personal issues, the Lord loves you and wants you to feel supported and celebrated for the service you have given to Him.

- **Handling Social Pressure.** Some of your friends at home may not have the same life goals as you have now. Handling social pressure can be an ordeal and may cause you to leave behind some friends you still cherish.

- **Finding an Eternal Companion.** This is a new goal you have as a returned missionary. You may be surprised at how you can implement the same finding and communication techniques you used on your mission to find and relate to that perfect someone in your life.

- **Becoming Anxiously Engaged.** This goal is more important now than it was on your mission. You should reflect on ways you can strengthen your ward and others in the gospel whether you have a church calling or not.

- **Hastening the Work as a Seasoned Warrior**. As a returned missionary, you have become an experienced and seasoned warrior fighting in the battle for souls. Your example can help others understand their responsibility to hasten the work.

BECOMING A SUCCESSFUL RETURNED MISSIONARY

Many missionaries during their mission ask: "How do I know if I am a successful missionary?" You may now ask: "How do I know if I am a successful returned missionary?" The answer to the former question is found at the end of Chapter 1 in *Preach My Gospel*, and, not surprisingly, the points comprising that same answer still apply now that you're home. Your full-time mission was only the beginning of your life's mission. The new creature you have become and all the skills that you learned as a full-time missionary will help you find success in that new mission on which you have now embarked.

Prologue for Parents

Steve and I nervously arrived at the building long before our first institute class for returned missionaries was going to start. We checked our computer and projector connections, made sure the sound was at the appropriate volume, and put our first roll sheet on a table in the back of the room for people to sign as they entered. We were not sure if anyone would come, since this was something new and different. We had been praying hard about this first lesson. We were hoping it would touch the hearts and minds of these young people and meet their needs.

At 7 p.m., only two or three returned missionaries had arrived. We started the introductions, found out where they served their missions, and how long they had been home. Soon, a few more walked in, and a few others ten minutes later. In about twenty minutes, twenty-five returned missionaries were sitting in the room. We taught our lesson on "What is your Purpose Now?" and enjoyed a lively discussion, with all members of the class contributing actively. We concluded and had a closing prayer. The returned missionaries continued to sit in their seats as if they did not want to leave. We had all felt the Spirit of the Lord throughout the meeting. For me, the class had felt like one of the many zone conferences we had enjoyed during our mission in Brazil. That familiarity was hard to leave.

As we milled around afterward, discussing our missions and where we had served, one sister came up to me wanting to talk. She had only been home from her mission for a week. She said, "Sister Richardson, thank you so much for this lesson. It's just what I needed to hear! I've been trying to figure out what I'm going to do now and this lesson gave me a lot of hope. I only wish I'd heard it yesterday!"

I was intrigued. I had to ask her, "I'm just curious—what happened yesterday?"

"Well, I've really been struggling, you know, trying to figure out what I should do now that I'm home. During the mission, I knew what I was doing every minute of every day. Since being home, I've really felt lost and alone. Yesterday, I just broke down. I went to my father in tears, and I cried in his arms. Then, I asked him, 'Dad, what should I do?' My dad looked at me with tears in his eyes and stumbled over his words, 'Dear, I don't know how to help you.'"

As this young sister told me her story, my heart went out to both her and her father. All I could think about was the frustration and hopelessness her poor father must have felt as he held his righteous returned missionary daughter in his arms. She had obviously been taught and prepared to serve a full-time mission. Yet, he did not know how to help her with her next transition—how to be a righteous, fulfilled returned missionary.

Returned missionaries are a high priority for us. We have enjoyed working with them for many years in church callings. Steve released hundreds of returned missionaries as a stake president and presided over the Brazil São Paulo South Mission from 2008 to 2011. I had the privilege of being his companion and support for about 450 missionaries who we still care about deeply and try to follow up with regularly.

We are also the parents of twelve children. Eight of our children have served full-time missions, and a couple of our children still at home are preparing to go on missions, along with our many grandchildren. We have experienced the joys and frustrations of helping returned missionaries come back home and return to "normal" society. Our current calling is to watch over, teach, and help the returned missionaries within the Alpine Utah YSA Stake boundaries.

We love returned missionaries!

Eternal principles can help returned missionaries and their families during their transition home even though each returned missionary's circumstance is different. This book is full of suggestions. You will need to pray and fast for divine guidance as you strive to find out which of these suggestions would be the best fit for you and your family. You may find these suggestions inspire you with new ideas to try, for the Lord will "direct your hearts into the love of God"[1] as you and your returned missionary work together.

The chapters of this book were outlined in the "Prologue for Returned Missionaries." Each chapter begins with a section written directly to returned missionaries. That section is followed by another section directed to their parents, and, in some cases, an additional section has been included with suggestions for other family members. We have added a final chapter specifically written to parents who are preparing other sons and daughters for missionary service entitled "For Parents of Future Missionaries."

Quotes from returned missionaries are placed at the beginning of each section for missionaries and quotes from parents are placed at the beginning of each section for parents. Many people were willing to share their thoughts and ideas with us.[2] We are thankful for the opportunity to learn from them and their experiences and we hope you will learn from their stories as well.

In the sections to parents, the following topics will be discussed to assist you in your essential role during this crucial period of your son or daughter's life:

- **Coming home.** After the initial excitement of coming home wears off, your returned missionaries will be left with the question, "Now what?" You still have power and influence in directing and supporting them during this important transition.

- **Fulfilling your eternal purpose.** Missionaries recite their purpose often during their mission. You need to help them understand that their purpose has not changed. The key to a successful transition home is the realization that the missionary purpose is really their life's purpose!

- **Keeping the glow.** You now have the opportunity to learn from your returned missionaries. Encourage them to continue to be gospel scholars, to pray continually, and to let the Spirit radiate from their countenances. You should practice this yourself, too! Hopefully, some of their glow will rub off on you and your family.

- **Using *Preach My Gospel* forever.** Read and study *Preach My Gospel* before your missionaries return home and follow up with them on their continued use of this book, which has become their dear friend.

- **Dealing with family changes.** Your family may have changed a lot over the past eighteen months or two years. You will want to communicate these changes to your missionaries and give them some time to handle these changes. If there has been a death in the family, support your missionaries while they grieve, since they probably will not have had a chance to do so while on their mission.

- **Rising above challenges.** As soon as your missionaries return home, give them a priesthood blessing. Interview them to find out how they are doing spiritually and emotionally. Missionaries are accustomed to regular interviews and you may want to consider continuing this practice during their transition home.

- **Coming home early.** As a parent of a returned missionary who came home early, you may not feel prepared for this unexpected pause or ending to your son or daughter's mission. Understanding how to help your son or daughter is an important step in their healing process. You may need some time to heal, too. Realize that the Lord loves you, and wants you, as well as your child, to feel supported during this time.

- **Handling social pressure.** You will need to help your missionaries deal with pressures from friends (and even from siblings) to return to activities and behaviors of the past that they have left far behind. They may feel tempted to return to the person they were before if not encouraged and strengthened.

- **Finding an eternal companion.** This is the most important decision your returned missionaries will make. As a parent, support and encourage them in their decisions, but don't pressure.

- **Becoming anxiously engaged.** You need to become an example to your returned missionaries of being anxiously engaged, rather than being critical of the things you think they are not doing. This includes being an example of regular temple attendance and inviting them to join you.

- **Hastening the work as a seasoned warrior.** These young warriors may need your help in binding up their wounds and strengthening their resolve. You need to be an example to them of a covenant keeper, which will keep both you and them safe from the evils of the world.

- **For Parents of Future Missionaries.** You may have other children who are preparing for full-time missionary service. This chapter provides additional ideas of how to prepare them emotionally, physically, socially, and spiritually for a mission.

USING *PREACH MY GOSPEL*

Preach My Gospel is the book missionaries study diligently during their mission. This inspired book can also help you prepare for your missionary's return. Spend some time reading and studying it before they come home, and after! As you read and study its pages, you will be reminded that "God loves you and all His children. He is anxious to support you in your practical and specific challenges. You have been promised inspiration to know what to do and have been given the power to do it. . . . He will shower His blessings upon you through the gift of the Holy Ghost. He asks that you remain worthy of this gift and that you ask, seek, and knock."[3] May the Lord bless you with the understanding and inspiration from the Holy Ghost to know how to best serve your returned missionaries.

NOTES

1. 2 Thessalonians 3:5
2. The stories told in this book come from returned missionaries from our mission and returned missionaries who have taken our institute class. Some stories combine the experiences of multiple missionaries. Generally, names have been changed, but all of the stories have happened to real returned missionaries.
3. *Preach My Gospel* (Salt Lake City, Utah: The Church of Jesus Christ of Latter-day Saints, 2004), 89.

Coming home was really difficult. You have a mind-set for two years. You come home and you are asked to keep that mind-set, yet, at the same time, you are asked to go into a whole new environment, so it's very difficult.

➤ RETURNED MISSIONARY ELDER

Coming Home

NOW WHAT?

So, you're home. You've been a missionary. The one goal you worked so hard to accomplish is complete. Long before your mission, you worked hard to prepare yourself to serve the Lord. If you grew up in the Church, you probably wanted to serve as a missionary from a young age. You attended Primary and sang the words "We are as the army of Helaman"[1] with gusto. If you joined the Church as a teenager or a young adult, you probably watched the missionaries who baptized you and thought how much you would like to serve others, as they served you.

Either way, you probably envisioned yourself as a future missionary becoming like those armies of Helaman, preparing for a spiritual battle, and becoming part of a battalion of righteous missionaries who would bring the gospel of Jesus Christ to the world. You gave your all to hasten His work and were assisted along the way with the help of your family, priesthood leaders, and teachers.

Now what?

What are your goals for the next two years?

What is your duty and purpose now that you've returned home?

Elder L. Tom Perry envisioned the amazing power of your influence as a returned missionary when he declared, "What we need is a royal army of returned missionaries reenlisted into service."[2] He saw you together with your fellow returned missionaries as a great force for good, strengthening the Church and moving the work forward as seasoned warriors who know how to do missionary work and to be successful on the front lines of sharing the gospel with others. Your mandate from the Lord is to become a part of that royal army, just as you looked forward to serving like the armies of Helaman while you were on your mission.

A HOMECOMING FOR SAM

Sam loved his mission. He loved everything about it—the people, the food, the other missionaries, and his mission president. But he was coming to the end of his mission and his thoughts were starting to turn home. He had one week left of his mission. Today was his last P-day. His mother's last email contained a detailed summary of all the events his family was planning for the days following his homecoming. The bishop had already scheduled him to speak the first Sunday he came home. All his girlfriend Jenny could write about in recent letters was how it had seemed forever since she had snuggled close to him and felt his strong arms around her. (He could not help daydreaming a bit about Jenny.) He couldn't wait to eat a Big Mac and enjoy his mother's cooking rather than his companion's barely edible concoctions.

At the airport, Sam was greeted by his entire family with balloons, a homemade sign, a new baby nephew whom he had never met, and, of course, Jenny. He hugged them all like he never wanted to let them go.

Sam did not want to think about anything else, except about being home. The problem was that there was nothing else to think about. He didn't know what he was going to do, and he just couldn't seem to focus on future plans anyhow. Right now, all he could think about was Jenny, his own bed, a washer and dryer that really worked, and life without cockroaches. He would just take it easy for a while and then decide what he was going to do after sleeping for about two weeks. Wow, did that sound good!

After the excitement and events of the first week at home wore off, however, life started to become difficult. Jenny had changed. He had changed. They didn't seem to have much in common and their relationship was not the same as it used to be. His family had changed, too, and some of the things they wanted to do didn't interest him anymore. Without the constant organization, planning, and work-filled days of missionary service, he started to feel empty and without a purpose. He had never been a very good student before his mission, but now he actually enjoyed studying. He was worried it might be too late to be accepted into a college or university. He felt like he was just wasting time lying around the house all day.

His prayers and scripture study were neither as intense nor as uplifting as they were on his mission. He found his mind constantly returning to the same questions. Just what should he do with his life now? What was his purpose as a returned missionary? He wasn't sure.

COMING HOME CAN BE TOUGH

Sam's story is not original, nor is it very different from some of the events that you've probably experienced. On the mission, you may have felt great excitement (and maybe a little trepidation) thinking about your return home. Perhaps you imagined how wonderful it would be to sleep in your own bed, eat your mother's cooking, and see all of your old friends. Like Sam, your homecoming may also have been an unforgettable moment, filled with an overpowering mix of joy, love, and Spirit. However, as the weeks pass and the rush of emotion dies down, you may begin to feel unsettled in your new environment. You may feel uncomfortable with old friends and their standards and even uncomfortable with your own family. If you served in a different country, you may have difficulties speaking English and expressing your thoughts and feelings without slipping into your mission language.

That's okay! You need to acknowledge that this is normal and most returned missionaries feel the same way (even though they may not talk about it openly). You're not strange or weird or even unworthy if you have these feelings. They're normal!

Think back to the first months of your mission. Even though you were excited to be on the mission, you probably took a few months—perhaps as many as six months or even a year—to feel comfortable in your new surroundings with the new rules, new schedules, and new culture. You had a companion to get to know and maybe a new language to learn, too. It was tough, yet worth every effort.

The same is true with returning from your mission. Give yourself time, like you did at the beginning of your mission. You need to readjust to new rules, new schedules, and new surroundings. You need to decide how and when you will plan your time, how and to whom you will be accountable, and what your long- and short-term goals will be. You may feel like you have been thrust back into the world without any tools or a companion to help you. That is not true! You taught in the first lesson,

"Heavenly Father has provided us, His children, with a way to be successful in this life and to return to live in His presence."[3]

The Lord will be by your side now, just like He was on your mission.
The difference is that you are now a seasoned warrior whom the Lord can
trust to make righteous decisions. When you ask, seek, and knock, He
will be there because you "are to be taught from on high."[4] The principles
in the scriptures and in *Preach My Gospel,* which you used on your mission and which you taught to your investigators, are the key to success in
your own new life.

THE STRESS OF TRANSITIONS

Whenever we struggle with major transitions in our lives, we become
vulnerable to negative emotions such as depression, frustration, loneli-
ness, despair, and even anger. Psychologists and sociologists continue to
study the role of major life transitions on mental health and values. Most
of these studies focus on such transitions as job loss, divorce, retirement,
and widowhood, but you, as a returned missionary, are dealing with transitions that can be just as challenging to your own self-image and devel-
opment. You are dealing with the transitions of finding a job, finding a
direction in life, figuring out what to study at school and how to pay for
it all. On top of all that, you must find an eternal companion: the perfect
forever match for you. These pressures can have a significant influence on
your motivation and choices.

When you feel directed and purposeful, you will be able to maintain
the excitement you felt on your mission. If you do not have a purpose or
direction, you may find that you feel lost and unable to cope with the
transition of returning home. These stressors can create a need for outside
support and, sometimes, professional help.

Coming home affects each missionary differently. For some, coming
home is a great relief and a burden lifted. Such a reaction does not mean
that you were any less dedicated or hard working as a missionary; sometimes, it is the exact opposite. Maybe you have been so obedient and
hard-working that coming home is a necessary and needed stress reliever.
Some sociologists have observed that not all life transitions are inherently
stressful.[5] Instead, some transitions can actually bring relief rather than
additional tension.

For example, Allan was an assistant to the president for the last six
months of his mission. For the six months previous to that, he had helped

in the office working closely with his mission president as the financial clerk. He had enjoyed these leadership positions and had learned a great deal about leadership and caring for others, especially from the powerful example of his mission president. Yet coming home had been a tremendous relief for him. He felt as if a huge burden had been lifted off his shoulders. He looked forward to a week at home before he started school as a business major at a local university. He couldn't wait! He was excited to bring to his education all of the life lessons and professional leadership experience he had acquired on his mission.

ROLE EXITS

Changing roles in life can bring doubts and fears about where you belong and how you should act. The role of a missionary is very demanding and all-encompassing. Now you have to figure out what your new role is in the Church and in the world.

Tom used to prefer playing video games over doing anything else. Before leaving on a mission, he told his family and friends that he was done with school. He was happy to just get by in an easy day job that would allow him to play video games all night. Then he was called to serve in the Helsinki Finland Mission. Being away from video games was really hard on Tom at first. He almost came home a couple of times while he was serving in the MTC. He also felt awkward speaking in front of people. He had never taught anybody anything before (except how to kill an alien while playing Halo).

When he first arrived in Finland, he could not understand anything happening around him, even after his two months of language training at the MTC. He hated that feeling and decided he would learn Finnish as quickly as he could. So he studied hard for the first time in his life. He was surprised to find that he enjoyed languages. Even studying the scriptures became more enjoyable as he studied them in another language. He gained an immense love for the Finnish people, too. He began to realize how much he had missed by not exerting himself intellectually to a greater degree before his mission.

As Tom started thinking about returning home, he did not have any plans. Before his mission, he had never thought about going to college and he felt ashamed about how he had told his parents and friends he was happy to be done with school. His feelings had changed and he now wanted to go to college and maybe even study other languages. He

5

worried that his parents would not believe him or have faith in his new-found abilities and that his friends would just make fun of him. As a missionary, he felt comfortable with his new talents. After his mission, he was worried about how he would be able to maintain them.

Studies have confirmed that a person who leaves a role and becomes "an ex" often goes through a process of self-doubt, a search for another role, and a creation of a new identity.[6] Hopefully, your search for a new identity after your mission will lead you on paths of self-discovery that will enable you to become a better and stronger person than you were before your mission, with a better vision of what your adult life as a disciple of Christ can and will be.

FINDING YOUR IDENTITY

As a stake president, Steve had the missionaries from the stake come to our home the day they returned to be released from their callings as full-time missionaries. He would first interview them and then have them report to him about their missions. After they were done talking, he would ask them to take off their missionary tag and carefully look at the two names that were on it one last time before putting it away. For most missionaries, this final look at their name tag was a very moving and emotional moment, especially as they contemplated their full-time service to Jesus Christ. They often choked up a bit and even the manliest missionaries would shed tears with the sense of loss they felt as they took off the badge that symbolized their role as a full-time servant of the Lord.

Two weeks ago, Diana returned from her mission. Today was the first day she had nothing to do. She looked forward to rereading some of her missionary journals and reading scriptures for more than just ten minutes. As she sat down to look at her missionary things, her missionary tag fell to the floor. She picked it up and tears sprang to her eyes, which caught her by surprise.

She began to think about how different her life was now to what it had been just two weeks ago. She had a room all to herself without having to share it with three other sisters, she had all the food she could ever want at any time, day or night, she could listen to any music she wanted, and she could even watch television. Yet, she felt empty inside—emptier since looking at her name on her missionary tag. How she wished she were back in Costa Rica!

She decided to place her tag on the inside pocket of her purse so she could still feel it and look at it every so often, even though others could not see it. She missed being a missionary and felt a little lost about what the Lord wanted her to do now.

After taking off that badge, you may also feel like you need to take on a whole new identity and become a different person from who you were during the mission. This search for a new identity is a necessary part of the transition home. Some may feel like they need to experiment with different adult paths until they find the one that feels right, while others may feel they don't need to change or experiment much at all.

If you have found yourself engaged in such a quest, you must remember that a fundamental part of your identity has not changed, nor will it ever change. You have been, are, and forever will be a servant of Jesus Christ. You worked hard during your mission and you must continue to work hard now. You may have different key indicators in your life, but your purpose of inviting yourself and others to come unto Christ will remain constant.

While you were on your mission, you had the scriptures, *Preach My Gospel*, the *Missionary Handbook,* and the *Missionary Daily Planner.* These tools helped you organize and direct yourself toward achieving your long-term goals as well as your daily and weekly key indicator goals. Your daily schedule told you when to wake up, eat breakfast, study your scriptures, work, return home, plan, and, go to bed. Now you need to figure out a new daily schedule, new key indicators, and new goals to direct your life.

As you embark on this new journey, remember that you are not alone! You have parents, priesthood leaders, other returned missionaries, and the Spirit to help you figure things out. The Lord will not forsake you because you have been His servant. He has promised: "Behold, I sent you out to testify and warn the people. . . . He that seeketh me early shall find me, and shall not be forsaken."[7]

STAYING EXCITED!

You probably had strong feelings of excitement and expectation as you were preparing to leave on your mission. You were excited to serve the Lord. From the moment you received your call, people asked you, "Where are you going?" And no matter where you had been assigned to serve, they would shower you with positive acclamations about your upcoming experience.

The day before our son Adam left for the Buenos Aires, Argentina Missionary Training Center, he said, "I'm excited to go! I'm really happy to have this opportunity to serve the Lord. I know I will grow a lot and I know it will be a lot of work learning a new language and a new culture, but, in the end, it will all pay off. I can't wait!"

As a newly returned missionary, you likely experienced a similar burst of excitement and flurry of activity at your homecoming, too. Family members may have come to visit whom you hadn't seen since before you left. Everyone was celebrating your return home. Your family may have even gone on a vacation. You spoke in sacrament meeting in your home ward and you may have also been asked to be a companion speaker with high councilors throughout the stake. During this initial period after your return, you could still easily feel that you were fulfilling your purpose as you shared your experiences and testimony with others. You felt appreciated and needed.

Excitement is a wonderful emotion that needs to be nurtured or the emotion vanishes. Joseph Smith wrote, "Excitement has almost become the essence of my life. When that dies away, I feel almost lost. When a man is reined up continually by excitement, he becomes strong and gains power and knowledge; but when he relaxes for a season, he loses much of his power and knowledge."[8] Just as the Prophet Joseph described, when the excitement of coming home dies away, you may feel lost. If you begin to relax for too long, you may begin to lose the power and knowledge you had while you were a missionary. Those feelings of loss may bring negative emotions, which are in sharp contrast to the positive feelings you felt on your mission. Because of this contrast, you may begin to feel guilt or frustration, and question whether the influence of the Spirit of the Lord is still in your life.

You don't have to lose your excitement for the gospel, however. Instead, your enthusiasm for the gospel can become even stronger! You can continue to rekindle the fire in your bones talked about by the prophet, Jeremiah. He had been told to stop preaching the gospel, but he could not do it. Jeremiah exclaimed, "But his word was in mine heart as a burning fire shut up in my bones, and I was weary with forbearing, and I could not stay."[9] The weariness that Jeremiah describes when he stopped preaching the gospel may be what you feel when you come home and stop preaching the gospel.

So don't stop! Keep the fire burning! Be like Jeremiah and continue to fulfill your purpose, preaching the gospel and inviting yourself, your family, your loved ones, your friends, your coworkers, and even strangers on the street to come unto Christ and to live the doctrine of Christ!

Suggestions for Parents

When I came home, I had a good mission president who said, "I want you to realize that you will have expectations—but this is going to be very difficult." That was very helpful to know that coming home was going to be a difficult experience. I just remember when my three sons returned home, they had that 'deer in the headlights' look like most returned missionaries do. All of a sudden, they'd say, "Wow, what do I do now?" And I was able to say, "You know what . . . try to realize that you're in a transition. We'll give you all the love and support you need. We'll always be here if you need someone to talk to." My sons all seemed to transition well.

➤ FATHER OF RETURNED MISSIONARIES

As parents, we typically sacrifice and work hard in order to make our children's goal of going on a mission a reality. We take them to church on Sundays and to young men and young women activities. We have family home evenings, family scripture study, and family prayer in our homes. We work alongside our future missionaries to prepare them for the rigors of their upcoming service. Together, we also look forward to the day when our missionaries will complete their mission and return home with honor and celebration.

We want the best for our children. We look forward to their achievements and try to shield them from the stresses and trials of this world. Preparing for a mission is usually the biggest challenge our children have faced in their lives so far. Many parents are surprised when coming home becomes an even bigger challenge for many returned missionaries.

HOMECOMING—A PARENT'S PERSPECTIVE

Eric was our first missionary, and I remember vividly the day he came home from his mission in Guatemala. Perhaps some of you parents (especially mothers) can relate to the feelings I experienced.

Even though the Seattle sky was cloudy and grey as usual, I smiled up at the sky as if it were sunny and blue. My son was coming home from his mission! I could not wait to see his face again, wrap my arms around him, look into his eyes to make sure he was all right, and have him under my roof once more. Our family had faithfully read his letters every week, writing him back in return, and we enjoyed the humorous and spiritual stories Eric had shared with us during his two years of service, but I felt there were many other stories he may not have told us. I was looking forward to discussing them with him and finding out all the details he had been reticent to tell me while he was away from home.

We had also had our twelfth baby while he was on his mission—actually, while he was in the MTC. Deborah was now almost two years old and she had never met her older brother. I was looking forward to having these two get to know each other. Since it was the end of January, we would have Eric home with us for three glorious months before he went back to Brigham Young University for spring term.

All of the children held up the sign we had made together the night before. It read: "Welcome Home Eric!" in a combination of marker pen and crayon patterns, including scribbled embellishments added by the baby. We were a large group watching intently as each person came into the baggage claim area at Sea-Tac Airport. Finally, I spotted his familiar brown eyes. Eric's face lit up as he recognized us, and he started running toward us. He caught the baby and me in his strong arms. I didn't remember him being so tall or looking so much like a grown man. Tears streamed down my face as I kissed his cheek and held him close.

The emotionality of that day still resonates in my heart. I had no idea when Eric walked off the plane that he would have such a difficult time transitioning to "normal" life with his family. I thought it would be such a great time for him. In many ways, his first weeks home were wonderful. We listened to his missionary stories with rapt attention. He tried to make sure that he spent quality time with each of his younger siblings, taking them out for ice cream, picking them up after school, watching their sports games, and doing finger dances with them in the car to the sound track of *My Best Friend's Wedding*.

Initially, he had a hard time finding a job, so he spent long periods of time alone while everyone else was working, going to school, or participating in extra-curricular activities. When I was home, he would follow me around because he missed having a companion. I enjoyed his company and liked to hear his missionary stories.

He did not have a ward calling because the bishop felt he was leaving for school too soon. Everyone wanted him to take it easy. Yet he had been used to such a full and busy schedule for the past two years. His life on the mission had been overflowing with leadership responsibilities, teaching the gospel, and working with investigators and members. After being constantly busy for two years, the inactivity and idleness of home life were spiritually deadening to him.

He missed Guatemala and speaking Spanish, and he constantly thought about returning back to his mission. If home life was like this, he did not want it. All he wanted was to go back to his old life as a missionary. The only thing that kept him going during this time was the hope that when he returned to school, he would feel more fulfilled and ready to take on his new life as a returned missionary.

Gratefully, Eric made it through that difficult time, gradually regaining purpose and direction in his life as he met and married a wonderful young woman, finished school, and landed a great job. Today, he is a successful husband, father, church leader, and professional. Looking back, however, I wish I had known then what I know now about how to help returned missionaries through that transition. I could have made things so much better—both for him and for me!

The purpose of the following chapters is to pass on all that we have experienced and learned about this critical time for returned missionaries in the hope that the experience both for you and for your missionary will be a successful one. We are grateful to have benefitted greatly from the input and experiences of so many others and acknowledge their significant contribution to this effort.

THE POWER OF PARENTS

As we have spoken with parents of missionaries, we have been impressed with their openness and frankness about their concerns over the homecoming of their sons and daughters. As we have spoken with their missionaries after they returned home, we have found consistently that those missionaries wanted and needed their parents to have that same level of openness and frankness with them. As their parents, you must talk with them openly, expressing your love and concern for them, and asking them about their feelings and the challenges they are facing. Most importantly, however, you must be a good listener to their ready answers.

They need to feel that they can come to you about anything and that they can trust you to listen, understand, and help appropriately.

When your missionaries return home, they will often ask "Now what?" You have more power than you realize in helping them answer that question. Through encouragement, not coercion, you can help guide your returned missionaries to make better choices, choices that will continue to kindle their excitement for the gospel. Your love and advice can help shape and mold their feelings and understanding, providing direction for their future goals and purpose. Feeling your constant love and support, they will begin to see how their mission was only the beginning of their long-distance race for eternal life as they strive to endure to the end.

NOTES

1. Janice Kapp Perry, "We'll Bring the World His Truth," in *Children's Songbook* (Salt Lake City, Utah: The Church of Jesus Christ of Latter-day Saints, 1989), 172–73.

2. L. Tom Perry, "The Returned Missionary," *Ensign,* November 2001.

3. *Preach My Gospel* (Salt Lake City, Utah: The Church of Jesus Christ of Latter-day Saints, 2004), 31.

4. Doctrine and Covenants 43:16.

5. Blair Wheaton, "Life Transitions, Role Histories, and Mental Health," *American Sociological Review*, vol. 55, no. 2 (April 1990), 209–23.

6. Helen R. F. Ebaugh, *Becoming an Ex: The Process of Role Exit* (Chicago, Illinois: University of Chicago Press, 1988), 247; Linda K. George, "Sociological Perspectives on Life Transitions," *Annual Review of Sociology*, vol. 19 (1993), 353–73.

7. Doctrine and Covenants 88:81, 83.

8. Joseph Smith, *History of the Church of Jesus Christ of Latter-day Saints*, vol. 5, (Salt Lake City, Utah: Deseret News, 1909), 389.

9. Jeremiah 20:9.

Don't call us "weird" when we come home. I know I felt different when I came home. But, at the same time, I definitely was a different person. So, it takes some getting used to. It took some getting used to for us, as missionaries—changing and adapting. It's just going to take some getting used to for everyone else to change and adapt to our new lifestyle and standards. All the support you can give us is welcome.

› RETURNED MISSIONARY ELDER

Everybody changes on the mission and you can't go back to who you were before, but you always need to remember you've changed and remember who you are now.

› RETURNED MISSIONARY SISTER

Fulfilling Your
Eternal Purpose

WHAT IS MY PURPOSE NOW?

You, along with almost every other returned missionary, may be asking yourself this question. During zone and district meetings, you often recited your missionary purpose: "Invite others to come unto Christ by helping them receive the restored gospel through faith in Jesus Christ and His atonement, repentance, baptism, receiving the gift of the Holy Ghost, and enduring to the end."[1] These words became your mantra to guide you through your missionary experience.

Striving to internalize and live the missionary purpose for the period of your service has changed you. You became a new person with new habits and a solid foundation of testimony, faith, and action. By learning to live your purpose, which consists exactly of the five points of the doctrine of Christ, you created a sure foundation upon which the rest of your life is to be based.

So, what is your purpose now? It is the same! You must now take the areas of focus in your post-mission life (for examples, school, work, courtship, service, personal devotions) and place them squarely on this new foundation of the doctrine of Christ. Doing so will infuse all these aspects of your life with the proper purpose and direction so that you will never return to the person you were before. With this new foundation firmly established, you are set to become a better student, a better worker, a better friend, a better son or daughter, and a better disciple of Christ.

YOUR PURPOSE: THE DOCTRINE OF CHRIST

Robert had not really cared much about the Church before going on a mission. He had a difficult time at school, and his parents and siblings were on his back so much about his poor grades that he did not even like talking to them. He felt that all they did was put him down. He went to church infrequently. After a period of some personal change and preparation, he decided to go on a mission—not only because he felt it was the right thing to do but also because he wanted to get away from his family constantly nagging him about his life. As he served his mission, however, everything changed. He caught the vision of what his purpose on earth was. He returned home determined to be a better student, a more loving son, and an active member of his ward. He did not want to return to being the person he was before his mission. Even though his family initially treated him as the same person he had been before the mission, he remained determined to be who he had become and change their perspective of him through his actions. Today, he continues to be a fully active and engaged member of his ward and family. He is living the doctrine of Christ!

As a missionary, you testified that the Book of Mormon contains the fullness of the gospel, or the doctrine of Christ. Its pages are replete with explanations of the only way "whereby man can be saved in the kingdom of God."[2] The three chapters in the Book of Mormon that focus on this doctrine more than any others are:

- 2 Nephi 31
- 3 Nephi 11
- 3 Nephi 27

Your mission president focused your attention on these chapters to help you understand your purpose and the process by which you could successfully bring others to Christ. Now that you're home, you must continue to study these chapters and ask yourself, "How can I apply these principles in my life and in the lives of those around me?" Offer to teach your family and friends a family home evening lesson on this topic, and help them understand how they can apply this doctrine in their lives more effectively.

In 2 Nephi 31, Nephi explains to his people how their obedience to these principles will affect future generations.[3] He prophesies that the gospel will be restored in the latter-days to the Gentiles and then invites us all—the people of his time as well as the Gentile members of the latter-day church—to follow these plain and simple parts of the gospel plan:

> Wherefore, my beloved brethren, I know that if ye shall follow the Son, with full purpose of heart, acting no hypocrisy and no deception before God, but with real intent, repenting of your sins, witnessing unto the Father that ye are willing to take upon you the name of Christ, by baptism—yea, by following your Lord and your Savior down into the water, according to his word, behold, then shall ye receive the Holy Ghost; yea, then cometh the baptism of fire and of the Holy Ghost; and then can ye speak with the tongue of angels, and shout praises unto the Holy One of Israel. . . . And I heard a voice from the Father, saying: Yea, the words of my Beloved are true and faithful. He that endureth to the end, the same shall be saved.[4]

This is the doctrine of Christ: "this is the way; and there is none other way nor name given under heaven whereby man can be saved."[5]

The Savior himself testified of this doctrine when He visited the Nephites. After they all came forward, one by one, thrusting their hands into His side and touching the nail prints in His hands and feet, He gave them the authority to baptize and taught them how to perform the ordinance so that there would be no disputations about how to do it.

He then proclaimed, "Behold, verily, verily, I say unto you, I will declare unto you my doctrine."[6] His doctrine did not change from the teachings of Nephi almost six hundred years earlier, and His doctrine is the same today. He promised the Nephites, "whoso buildeth upon this buildeth upon my rock, and the gates of hell shall not prevail against them."[7] Then, He warned, "whoso shall declare more or less than this, and establish it for my doctrine, the same cometh of evil, and is not built upon my rock."[8] This is the same promise and warning to us today!

Not coincidentally, the Savior used these same statements about building on His rock when he instituted the sacrament among the Nephites. Referring to this sacred ordinance, he declared: "And I give unto you a commandment that ye shall do these things. And if ye shall always do these things blessed are ye, for ye are built upon my rock. But whoso among you shall do more or less than these are not built upon my rock, but are built upon a sandy foundation."[9]

In the former case, Jesus taught that if we build our lives on His doctrine, we build on His rock. In this latter case, He declared that if we always partake of the sacrament worthily, we are built on His rock. Make this relationship between the doctrine of Christ and the sacrament a topic of special personal study and application in your life. Ponder Elder James J. Hamula's statement in general conference: "Through the sacramental prayers, we express our acceptance of this doctrine of Christ and our commitment to live according to it."[10]

Each day we build our faith as we pray, study the scriptures, serve others, and keep the commandments. We strive to repent as we work to eliminate bad behaviors and habits and replace them with good ones. As we come to sacrament meeting having thus prepared ourselves, we partake of the sacrament and thereby renew our baptismal covenant with the Lord, committing to follow Him more earnestly. In return, we receive the promise that we will "always have his Spirit to be with [us]."[11] We then continue on our journey of endurance to the end throughout the next week: building our faith, repenting, and returning once again to renew our baptismal covenant and to receive His Spirit. Walking this path each week is exactly how we live the doctrine of Christ. Thus, the ordinance of the sacrament is the anchor that securely fastens our lives to the rock of our Redeemer.

Each week, make the sacrament the centerpiece of your efforts to live the doctrine of Christ. Reflect on your efforts over the previous week to continue to build your faith and to repent, and then promise the Lord that you will strive to do better in the coming week. As you do this with real intent, you will most certainly feel the witness of the Holy Ghost confirming the Lord accepts your commitment and your efforts, imperfect as they are. After you have done this for yourself, ponder about whom you could reach out to, as you continue to invite others to come unto Christ and walk this same path.

Many additional insights regarding the importance of living the doctrine of Christ may be gleaned from the Savior's teachings during His visit to the Nephites. As he began His Sermon on the Mount, he added another Beatitude: "And again, more blessed are they who shall believe in your words because that ye shall testify that ye have seen me, and that ye know that I am. Yea, blessed are they who shall believe in your words, and come down into the depths of humility and be baptized, for they shall be visited with fire and with the Holy Ghost, and shall receive a remission of their sins."[12] In other words, blessed are those who live the doctrine of Christ!

Not only was His doctrine an essential part of His first instruction to the Nephites, but Mormon concludes the report of His visit by quoting His words directed to all of us: "Turn, all ye Gentiles, from your wicked ways; and repent of your evil doings . . . and come unto me, and be baptized in my name, that ye may receive a remission of your sins, and be filled with the Holy Ghost, that ye may be numbered with my people who are of the house of Israel."[13] Once again, the command is to live His doctrine now and forever!

MAKE A GAME PLAN

While reading this chapter, perhaps you've been thinking, "I know all that. My mission president taught me this a million times. I get it! But real life is challenging. I need some practical advice on how to continue with my purpose. On the mission, I had *Preach My Gospel*, my planner, my missionary handbook, and my companion to help me—now where can I turn for help and guidance?"

Well, first of all, your right to receive inspiration and guidance from the Holy Ghost has not changed at all. The Holy Ghost can be your companion now. After all, he was a companion to you on your mission. More than at any other time in your life, you need, and the Lord wants to give you, inspiration from this divine source as you make decisions that will affect the rest of your life and into the eternities. (This will be discussed in more detail in Chapter 6.)

Furthermore, you can still have a paper or digital planner, and you certainly still have the Book of Mormon and *Preach My Gospel* to read and study. These two books formed the bedrock of your study as a missionary, and they should continue in this role even now. The applicability of *Preach My Gospel* to post-mission life is the topic of Chapter 4. Family members and friends can be an important and additional support to you. Many of these people have been through this same transition themselves.

Priesthood leaders also have inspired and practical ideas to help you apply your purpose in your post-mission life. Listening to past general conferences is a great place to start finding such suggestions. In the October 2013 General Conference, Elder S. Gifford Nielsen taught all members to make a personal game plan with the Lord to determine how to accomplish our purpose in our daily life. He explained, "I wanted to put my excitement and my faith in Jesus Christ into action. When I played football, I thought in terms of game plans. There was no question going into a contest that if our team was prepared with the right plays, we were going to be successful. . . . Since we are all on the Lord's team, do we each have our own winning game plan? Are we ready to play?"[14]

He suggested a game plan of three practical suggestions you can follow each day to remember your purpose:

1. "Specifically pray to bring someone closer to the Savior and His gospel every day."[15]

2. "Pray for the missionaries serving in your area and their investigators by name every day."[16] You may also include the missionaries and investigators from your mission.

3. "Invite a friend to an activity in or out of your home."[17] Becoming a friend and serving others as Christ would is the same way you were able to soften hearts on your mission. You can continue doing those same things now as a returned missionary.

The three points of the above plan are specifically about reaching out to others, as you did on your mission, and helping them come to Christ. However, you may feel, as many returned missionaries do, that the focus of your life now is on school, work, and courtship. Your life seems more self-centered and doesn't seem to fit well within the context of your purpose.

The resolution of this seeming contradiction is found in understanding that these activities establish an absolutely essential framework, within which your eternal purpose can be fulfilled most effectively. The key to keep in mind is that the purpose of your schooling and your subsequent vocation is to support your marriage and family, and that your family is the divinely appointed structure through which you, your spouse, your children, your grandchildren, and all your posterity are guided along the path leading to eternal life and exaltation. As you keep the proper perspective of these activities, focusing each day on living the doctrine of Christ and continuing to serve and lift others, you will find that all these things fit beautifully into the great whole of bringing to pass "the immortality and eternal life of man."[18]

As you create and implement a plan to bring family, friends, and all those around you to Christ, and as you prepare yourself so that you may continue to do this throughout your life, the Lord will direct your plan, helping it to work effectively, just like He did on your mission. Remember that following the principles of planning and goal-setting in Chapter 8 of *Preach My Gospel* will ensure the presence of divine guidance and produce results in accordance with the Lord's will. Wherever you go and whatever you do, ponder, and then listen to the Spirit as He directs you.

HELP PREPARE PROSPECTIVE MISSIONARIES

As a returned missionary, you have great power through your righteous example. People are looking at you to see what you will do now. This is especially true of your younger siblings. Encourage and support those around you to understand their eternal purpose. They may have the misconception that this purpose is only for full-time missionaries. Help them to understand that this is their purpose, too.

Andre enjoyed being a little different before his mission. He let his beautiful hair grow down to his waist—it was the envy of many his friends, especially the girls. He also enjoyed shooting guns, especially rifles, in competitions. Andre decided to become a full-time missionary, so he cut his hair and began to prepare spiritually to go on a mission. While on his mission, he was obedient to the mission rules and enjoyed living his purpose. After he returned home, he enjoyed being with his friends. He started shooting his rifle competitively again, but he decided to keep his hair missionary length.

Many of his friends asked him, "Why are you keeping your hair so short?" This question led to many significant discussions about obedience and how the mission had changed him inside and out. Keeping his hair short was an outward manifestation of the changes he felt inside because of his missionary service. He did not want those changes to leave, so he kept his hair short as a physical reminder. He became a powerful example to the young people in his ward and helped many of them to prepare to go on missions as well.

You may have younger siblings and friends who are thinking about going on missions, as well as active and inactive members in your ward who are of missionary age. As you consider where you should begin in your efforts to bring others to Christ now that you are home, you may want to concentrate on these young men and women. They will look to you as an example. You may want to try Elder Nielsen's plan of praying for them by name, praying for opportunities to bring them closer to the Savior, and asking them to join you at church activities as well as at other positive, wholesome activities.

DO YOU LOVE ME?

The Apostle Peter had been on a mission for three years as he served and was taught by the Savior. After the Savior's death, Peter was unsure about what he was supposed to do. He returned home to begin his life once more as a fisherman on the Sea of Galilee. After one long and unsuccessful night of fishing, the resurrected Savior appeared on the shore to Peter and those who were with him. The Savior's appearance was not known to the men as He directed them to cast their net on the other side of their boat. Following that advice, they could not draw in the net because of the multitude of fish they had caught. Peter instantly recognized the Savior as the person who had advised him to change the direction of his attempts to catch fish. With his characteristic enthusiasm and impulsiveness, he jumped from the boat and swam to shore to be with his beloved Master again. As He ate a dinner of bread and fish with His disciples, the Savior turned to Peter and asked him, "Lovest thou me more than these?"[19] The Savior was now asking Peter to change the direction of his life once more.

As with many returned missionaries, you may find the transition to post-mission life complex and problematic. Future plans do not always work out. You may try some things and find that your net comes up empty. Yet, if you sincerely ask the Lord for direction, He will help you know on which side of the boat to cast your net. As you seek His help with real intent, you must be willing to demonstrate your love for Him by sacrificing whatever is necessary to follow faithfully the promptings He provides. You may want to ask yourself regularly if you love the Lord more than your work, your education, your car, your "toys," or even your friends. Love for Him, demonstrated by unfailing willingness to follow Him, must be your first priority.

Elder Jeffrey R. Holland retold Peter's story with the insight that on Judgment Day each of us will probably be asked a similar question: "Did you love me?"[20] For, reminded Elder Holland, the first and greatest commandment is, "Thou shalt love the Lord thy God with all thy heart, and with all thy soul, and with all thy strength, and with all thy mind."[21] As a returned missionary, you must show your love to the Lord by remembering your purpose and by always being true to that purpose. Elder Holland further declared, "The call is to come back, to stay true, to love God, and to lend a hand. I include in that call to fixed faithfulness every returned missionary who ever stood in a baptismal font and with arm to the square said, 'Having been commissioned of Jesus Christ.' That commission was to have changed your convert forever, but it was surely supposed to have changed you forever as well."[22]

Suggestions for Parents

As they started to have experiences back in the real world every day, it was tough for them to hold on to the Spirit. A family needs to help their returned missionaries stay connected to the gospel, to something that would occupy their heart, rather than worrying about their hair or changing their manner of dress—help them stay with what they've learned those last important months of their life on their mission.

> ➤ MOTHER OF RETURNED MISSIONARIES

OUR PURPOSE AS PARENTS

At some point after coming home, your returned missionary may become very concerned or even depressed and ask you, "What am I supposed to do now? I don't know what to do! What is my purpose?" As their parent, you can be ready to answer, "Your purpose hasn't changed. You have the same purpose that you had on your mission! The purpose you recited on your mission should still be the mantra for your life now as it was while you were a full-time missionary."

Just as your returned missionary continues to have the purpose of inviting others to Christ, your purpose as a parent now most importantly includes inviting and helping your returned missionary to continue coming to Christ. With some slight rewording, we suggest that you consider making the following a statement of your purpose as it pertains to your son or daughter:

> Invite [my son/daughter] to come unto Christ by helping [him/her] receive the restored gospel through faith in Jesus Christ and His Atonement, repentance, [keeping his/her covenants], [using] the gift of the Holy Ghost, and enduring to the end.[23]

Of course, your example will speak more loudly than your words. The return of your missionary is in fact a blessed opportunity to review how you are living the doctrine of Christ in your life and how you might improve, and then to make those improvements together with your missionary. As they see you striving to improve and to live your purpose, they will do the same!

Suggestions for Families

FINDING THE DOCTRINE OF CHRIST IN THE BOOK OF MORMON

We had our missionaries do an activity that visually illustrated how the Book of Mormon truly contains the fullness of the gospel or doctrine of Jesus Christ. We bought each elder and sister a little box of colored pencils. Each color represented one point of that doctrine:

- Green was faith

- Red was repentance

- Blue was baptism

- Yellow was the gift of the Holy Ghost

- Orange was enduring to the end

Then, we all read the Book of Mormon in a short amount of time (two transfers, or three months). We underlined the text in the appropriate color every time we saw one of these concepts being taught or exemplified. At the next zone conference, all of us compared the colorful pages of our Book of Mormon.

This is a great activity to do together as a family. You may want to spend more than three months, but your family will be surprised at how enjoyable your reading will become as you try to find the doctrine of Christ in every page. This activity forcefully illustrates how the fullness of the gospel or doctrine of Jesus Christ permeates this inspired book.

NOTES

1. *Preach My Gospel* (Salt Lake City, Utah: The Church of Jesus Christ of Latter-day Saints, 2004), 1.
2. 2 Nephi 31:21.
3. Ibid.

4. 2 Nephi 31:13, 15.

5. 2 Nephi 31:21.

6. 3 Nephi 11:31.

7. 3 Nephi 11:39.

8. 3 Nephi 11:40.

9. 3 Nephi 18:12–13.

10. James J. Hamula, "The Sacrament and the Atonement," *Ensign,* November 2014.

11. Doctrine and Covenants 20:77.

12. 3 Nephi 12:2.

13. 3 Nephi 30:2.

14. S. Gifford Nielsen, "Hastening the Lord's Game Plan!" *Ensign,* November 2013.

15. Ibid.

16. Ibid.

17. Ibid.

18. Moses 1:39.

19. John 21:15.

20. Jeffrey R. Holland, "The First Great Commandment," *Ensign,* November 2012.

21. Luke 10:27.

22. Holland, "The First Great Commandment."

23. *Preach My Gospel,* 1.

When you're at the end of your mission, you kind of know, through the Spirit, what the Lord wants you to do just because of how hard you're working and how close you are to the Spirit. You kind of know where your life can end up and you're blessed to know what you can accomplish. So, I think when missionaries come home, they are ready to hit the ground running and they know what they want and what they can do. I would say—parents should have complete trust in that and just let them go. Just let them go and fulfill. They are on a spiritual high, so whatever they do, it will be good—their initial jump into life. So let them go and don't hold them back.

> RETURNED MISSIONARY ELDER

When it comes to spirituality—just don't take a day off. That is one thing I've found. Some days after your mission, you think, "Oh man, I'll just skip reading my scriptures this day." Then you might get kind of comfortable with that and you might skip two or three. You can feel a difference—because you are a returned missionary. As a returned missionary you are very sensitive to the Spirit. So skipping even a day can lead to a very crummy experience.

> RETURNED MISSIONARY ELDER

Keeping the Glow

When you first returned home, a discernible glow or spiritual aura shone around you. During your mission, you had tried to live as a servant of the Lord every minute of your life and it showed, even in your physical appearance. A mission changed you! You became a new person with new habits and a solid foundation of testimony, faith, and works. In order to maintain your new creature status, you need to continue those same habits, testimony, faith, and works you did on your mission without returning to the person you were before.

The Apostle Paul gave an eloquent description of people who become new creatures: "Wherefore, henceforth live we no more after the flesh; yea, though we once lived after the flesh, yet since we have known Christ, now henceforth live we no more after the flesh. Therefore if any man be in Christ, he is a new creature: old things are passed away; behold, all things are become new."[1]

I bought my son a new pair of jeans for school. He tried them on and said, "Thanks, Mom." He then went outside and rolled around in the grass and mud. I went outside and asked him what he was doing. He replied, "The kids would make fun of me if I came to school wearing perfect jeans. I need to break them in so they look right."

You may feel like you need to "dirty up" a bit in order to get back into normal society and hang out with your friends, so they don't make fun of you or call you "weird." They may want you to roll around in the worldly mud thinking that this will make you (and them) feel more comfortable. Don't do it!

While coming home is a new situation for both you and your friends and no one likes to feel strange or different, you can and must continue being the new person you've become. Lovingly strive to raise your friends up to your level rather than descending to a lower one. You will be fulfilling your purpose of bringing others to Christ, and you will all be better for it.

Moses had a similar problem when he returned to the children of Israel after talking to the Lord face to face. He came down from Mt. Sinai with the two tables of the law in his hands. He did not realize that "the skin of his face shone."[2] When Aaron, his brother, and the children of Israel (or his friends) saw Moses and realized he looked different, "they were afraid to come nigh him."[3] Moses' glow frightened his brother and his friends so much that he needed to "put a veil on his face"[4] when he talked with them.

You, as a returned missionary, do not need to feel embarrassed about your glowing countenance! Rather, as the Lord commanded, "Let your light so shine before men, that they may see your good works, and glorify your Father which is in heaven."[5]

KEEP YOURSELF UNSPOTTED FROM THE WORLD

Returning home from your mission, you may feel like you are rolling around in the mud a little bit. You walk off the airplane and immediately see so many things that are familiar, yet strange because you haven't been around them for a year or two. You don't need to wear missionary clothes anymore. You can sleep past 6:30 a.m. without feeling guilty (though you may still feel guilty for a little while). You can watch a video other than *The District* and friends or family may invite you to see the latest movie or to watch all the movies or play all the video games you missed while you were on your mission. You will probably feel uncomfortable with this, and you must realize that that feeling is the Spirit telling you that you don't have to do that (and perhaps shouldn't).

Elder Owens, a newly returned missionary said, "I think that is the hardest thing about coming back—finding out how your new self can fit. That first month I tiptoed back into the social scene. After sacrificing two years—which really isn't a sacrifice, becoming way, way better—it would be such a waste to throw that back."[6]

The scriptures give some very specific suggestions of things you can do to keep yourself unspotted from the world. These are activities you taught on your mission and did regularly. Now that you're home, you just need to continue doing them.

James, in his epistle to the early Christian saints, talked about pure religion and how to continue to be undefiled before God. He wrote: "Pure religion and undefiled before God and the Father is this, To visit the fatherless and widows in their affliction, and to keep himself unspotted from the world."[7] The Prophet Joseph Smith translated this verse by adding, "from *the vices of* the world."[8] As a missionary, you visited many in need. Continue visiting others in your callings, and as a home or visiting teacher, and continue to give service to others.

In latter-day revelation, the Lord taught: "And that thou mayest more fully keep thyself unspotted from the world, thou shalt go to the house of prayer and offer up thy sacraments upon my holy day."[9] Continue to go to church every Sunday and partake of the sacrament, pay your tithes and offerings, and keep the Sabbath day holy. These are habits you practiced and strengthened on your mission. You must continue working on them now that you are home.

FIND YOUR SPIRITUAL OASIS

Each of us needs to make choices in our lives between fitting in with the world and walking along the more solitary path that leads to eternal life. Lehi's dream provides us with the perfect example to follow. The righteous will traverse the path to the tree of life by holding fast to the rod of iron in spite of the large group of people in the great and spacious building, "both old and young, both male and female; and their manner of dress was exceedingly fine; and they were in the attitude of mocking and pointing their fingers towards those who had come at and were partaking of the fruit."[10]

While you are trying to follow the path, your friends and perhaps even your family may start to make fun of you or pressure you to change back to the person you were before your mission. They may not understand your desire to continue living such a strictly obedient life. They may say, "You're home! You don't need to follow those missionary rules anymore!" And you may begin to feel that your life would be much easier if you could join them in the "pleasures" of the world.

Realize that there are many good, uplifting things you can do now that you couldn't do while on the mission. With the spirit of discernment you developed on your mission, you will know what is good and what is not.[11] However, friends and even loved ones who repeatedly encourage and invite you to engage in activities that the Spirit whispers are spiritually destructive or not becoming of one who is truly converted, are those who do not have a complete understanding of the gospel in their lives. Perhaps they are still good people, who are simply "kept from the truth because they know not where to find it."[12] Or perhaps they know what's right, but still want to keep that summer cottage in Babylon[13] in their lives and want you to join them there to assuage the guilt from which they are unable to escape completely.

A metaphor similar to Lehi's dream is that of striving to reach an oasis in the middle of the desert. As we sometimes must pass through barren wastelands in our lives, our goal is to reach and abide in a beautiful, garden-like spot with lush, green vegetation, palm trees swaying in the breeze, cool and clear streams of living water flowing through it, and the bread of life spread about as manna on the ground. In the center of the oasis is a magnificent tree bearing fruit "which is most precious, which is sweet above all that is sweet, and which is white above all that is white, yea, and pure above all that is pure; and [if] ye shall feast upon this fruit even until ye are filled, . . . ye [shall] hunger not, neither shall ye thirst."[14]

As a returned missionary, you need to seek constantly such a spiritual oasis in your new life. This oasis may be your family's home, your apartment, or any place of spiritual refuge that is away from the enticements of the great and spacious building of the world. OASIS may also become an acronym to help you remember what you must do to keep yourself unspotted from the world and to fulfill your purpose, which is living and loving the doctrine of Christ.

OBTAIN THE WORD OF GOD

The "O" in OASIS is for **obtaining** the word of God. The Lord has said, "Seek not to declare my word, but first seek to obtain my word, and then shall your tongue be loosed; then, if you desire, you shall have my Spirit and my word, yea, the power of God unto the convincing of men."[15] He has also told you to "treasure up in your minds continually the words of life, and it shall be given you in the very hour that portion that shall be meted unto every man."[16]

In *Preach My Gospel*, you learned, "Study is an act of faith requiring the use of personal agency."[17] Sister Julie B. Beck said, "Some days I have a lot of time to contemplate the scriptures. Other days I reflect on a few verses. Just as eating and breathing sustain my physical body, the scriptures feed and give life to my spirit."[18] You may find it difficult to continue to study the way you did on your mission. Some days, you will only get a taste. Other days, you will find the time to feast until you are full. You need to plan daily scripture study even on busy days to keep your spirit healthy and strong.

To help others, you must first prepare yourself. You must obtain His word through daily prayer and study in order to be blessed by the presence of the Spirit, just as you did on your mission. Then, you will have the power of God to convince others of the truthfulness of the gospel, and thus continue to fulfill your purpose after your mission.

Two of our elders were teaching a woman who doubted the story of Joseph Smith and the Book of Mormon. Initially, she would not read the book. Then, she started reading a little bit and was blessed with some good feelings, but she wanted a spiritual confirmation that the gospel was true before she would be baptized. One of the elders wrote, "Sunday morning, she told me that she prayed fervently really asking the Lord if she was doing the right thing by being baptized. She randomly opened the Book of Mormon and fell upon 3 Nephi 30:2 which at the end tells us that we need to be baptized. She felt a peace in her heart and she gladly told us that she was more certain than ever that she had to be baptized and that Joseph Smith was a prophet because the Book of Mormon is true!"

In order for you to continue strengthening your testimony of the scriptures, you must continue studying and obtaining the word (just like you taught your investigators to do). If your scripture study has become stale and boring, try using some of the different ways of studying suggested in *Preach My Gospel* on pages 22 to 24. These include:

- Apply and live what you learn
- Search, ponder, and remember
- Use study resources
- See the big picture
- Explore the details

- Mark your scriptures[19]

The scriptures are full of the doctrine of Christ and reading them daily will enable you to remember who you really are and what your real purpose is upon the earth.

ASK FOR HEAVENLY FATHER'S HELP AND DIRECTION

The "A" in OASIS is for **asking** for Heavenly Father's help and direction. After you have prepared yourself spiritually, you must ask for His help. You cannot succeed without it. Many times, you will struggle as a returned missionary, just as you did as a full-time missionary. If you ask, the Lord will open the doors before you and put thoughts in your mind, words in your mouth, and people in your path whom you can help come unto Christ. As you help them, you will find the spiritual oasis you are seeking and they will join you there. The Lord has promised: "And all things, whatsoever ye shall ask in prayer, believing, ye shall receive."[20] Remember, you did this often on your mission! Continue to have that same faith you exercised in praying for help and direction daily.

Elder Silva and Elder Taylor had been having a really difficult day. They had been following up on contacts all day long and had not been allowed into even one house to give a lesson. The day turned into night. It started to rain—a cold steady drizzle that soaked them to the bone. They were determined that they would not give up or stop until they had found one new investigator. The elders huddled underneath a tree to pray. A thought came into Elder Silva's mind, and he suggested, "Hey, Elder Taylor, let's try singing hymns." Elder Taylor responded, "Let's do it . . . which house do you want to try first?" So the elders went door-to-door singing hymns in order to find a new investigator and teach a discussion. Elder Taylor wrote: "And then it happened—after a long series of rejections we found a man who said that he was an atheist, that he didn't believe in anything else outside himself. We taught him the plan of salvation and marked to come back. . . . I guess we showed the Lord that we were willing to face rejection after rejection and rain, dark and all other obstacles in order to find someone to teach—and He came through."

He will continue to come through for you, too, if you will ask Him.

SEEK FOR MISSIONARY EXPERIENCES

The first "S" in OASIS is for **seeking** for missionary experiences continually. After you ask for help, you can't sit around doing nothing! You need to put yourself in places and in situations where you can interact with and be an example to your family, your friends, and others. You can proactively seek opportunities to share spiritual experiences with them and bear testimony of the truths you know and love. As you continue to seek missionary experiences after returning home, you will feel the same powerful and comforting Spirit you felt for the last two years or eighteen months. Sharing the gospel is, after all, your continuing purpose!

The words of the hymn "Ye Elders of Israel" can continue to remind you to seek missionary experiences:

> Ye elders of Israel, come join now with me
> And seek out the righteous, where'er they may be—
> In desert, on mountain, on land, or on sea—
> And bring them to Zion, the pure and the free.[21]

Seeking for missionary experiences will enable you to continue feeling like a missionary. You may have given up your plastic missionary badge, but you can continue to have it "written . . . in fleshy tables of [your] heart."[22]

Ann had been home from her mission for about a month. She felt pretty well adjusted with her life at home, but missed the missionary experiences she had daily on her mission. Her parents had moved from southern California (where she had grown up) to Utah while she was on her mission. She decided to start searching for some of her old friends on Facebook to find out what they were doing. Soon, she found a girl with whom she had attended elementary school. They started chatting pretty regularly about their lives and their activities, hopes, and dreams.

Her friend began to ask her about her mission and all the Church activities she was attending constantly. Ann decided to send her friend a Book of Mormon in the mail and asked if she could send some missionaries to visit her. The missionaries gave her the lessons and Ann was able to answer her friend's questions on Facebook. One time, the missionaries even Skyped Ann into their missionary lesson. Ann was ecstatic when her friend messaged her on Facebook to say she had a baptismal date in just one week. Ann's experience of being a missionary on Facebook was incredibly rewarding and she is looking forward to interacting with others online who might be interested in the gospel message.

Elder Bednar talked at BYU Education Week about becoming a Facebook missionary. He said, "What has been accomplished thus far in this dispensation communicating gospel messages through social media channels is a good beginning—but only a small trickle. I now extend to you the invitation to help transform the trickle into a flood. Beginning at this place on this day, I exhort you to sweep the earth with messages filled with righteousness and truth—messages that are authentic, edifying, and praiseworthy—and literally to sweep the earth as with a flood."[23] You can be a part of that great flood in using social media to send the gospel message out into the world. You are an expert both at teaching the gospel and at using social media. What a perfect combination! Now you can hasten the work at home through Facebook, Twitter, Pinterest, and any other sites you use to communicate with others.

In the October 2013 General Conference, Elder Ballard invited members of the Church to "pray, personally and in your family, for missionary opportunities. . . . Ask Him for direction and then go and do as the Spirit prompts you."[24] He then clarified his invitation further: "We are not asking everyone to do everything. We are simply asking all members to pray, knowing that if every member, young and old, will reach out to just 'one' between now and Christmas, millions will feel the love of the Lord Jesus Christ." That effort did not have to end on December 25, 2013. This is an ongoing invitation for us to continually seek for "just one" person with whom to share the gospel throughout our lives. The Lord will surely help you as you obtain his word, ask for His help and direction, and then seek for missionary experiences, continuing the pattern you followed on your mission.

INVITE OTHERS TO COME UNTO CHRIST

The "I" in OASIS is for **inviting** others to come unto Christ. As discussed earlier, inviting others to come unto Christ is not only your missionary purpose, but the purpose of everyone, returned missionary or not, now and forever. One of the first duties young Aaronic priesthood holders receive when ordained to the office of deacon is "to warn, expound, exhort, and teach, and invite all to come unto Christ."[25] In inviting others, you follow the example of the Savior himself, who "sendeth an invitation unto all men, for the arms of mercy are extended towards them, and he saith: Repent, and I will receive you. Yea, he saith: Come unto me and ye shall partake of the fruit of the tree of life; yea, ye shall eat and drink of the bread and the waters of life freely."[26] He invites everyone to come to the spiritual oasis of eternal life!

You gave this same invitation to many on your mission, and now that you're home you must not stop! Sister Roberts and Sister Oliveira were trying to contact a reference. This was their third time trying to knock on the door and find this family. Finally, someone was home. The sisters discovered that the contact had moved from the address more than a year ago, but the couple who lived there welcomed them into their home. This couple already had their own copies of the Book of Mormon. Years ago, a coworker had given them these books. When the sisters asked the couple to mark 3 Nephi 11 and Moroni 10:3–5, their friend from years before had already marked these scriptures.

Now, this lovely couple was prepared and ready to read and pray about the truthfulness of the Book of Mormon and the restoration of the gospel. Sister Roberts wrote, "I thought about Doctrine and Covenants 4:4 and about how the Lord is preparing his children to receive the restored gospel. . . . I thought of this coworker, who so many years ago shared her testimony of the gospel and never got to see the fruits of her efforts. Now, this couple is ready for the gospel." Do not stop inviting others to come unto Christ. Even if you do not feel successful now, a missionary may later be able to open a door because of your efforts. The conclusion of Chapter 9 in *Preach My Gospel* states: "When people choose not to investigate the restored gospel, your work is not wasted. . . . Even when people do not accept the opportunity to learn the gospel, your service and words are evidence of God's love for them and may plant seeds that future missionaries and members of the Church will harvest."[27]

One of the easiest ways to invite others to know more about the gospel or to come back into activity is to always carry a couple of pass-along cards in your pocket, purse, or car. You can use them as thank-you cards at a restaurant, store, or barbershop—whenever someone provides a service of some kind to you. As you hand one to a person, all you have to do is ask, "Have you seen one of these before?" If they say yes, you can ask, "Oh, are you an active member of the LDS Church?" If they say they're LDS but less active, you can invite them to come back to church. If they say they've not seen the card or that they're not a member you can invite them to call and receive a free DVD. You may even offer to arrange for someone to deliver a DVD to their home if they would be comfortable giving you their address.

In any case, be sure to tell them you know that the Lord loves them and that they will feel that love as they watch the DVD or as they return to church. Of course, you have to sincerely mean it when you say this, and there is a simple key to being able to do that. Say a quick and silent prayer, asking the Lord to feel what He feels for that person. If done sincerely, you will feel His love for them, and your declaration will be authentic and powerful! The Spirit will also direct you so you will know what else to say in order to touch their heart and mind.

SAVE OTHERS AND YOURSELF

The final "S" in OASIS stands for **saving** others and yourself. As you **obtain, ask, seek,** and **invite**, you will **save** others, and as promised, you will experience that "great . . . joy with [them] in the kingdom of [your] Father!"[28] And you will save yourself as well![29]

The people you will save may be more than just strangers on the street. They may be members of your family, your children, dear friends, or your neighbors. Sometimes, you may think these people are beyond hope, and you may have stopped praying for them or inviting them to Church. The Lord has reminded us: "Unto such shall ye continue to minister; for ye know not but what they will return and repent, and come unto me with full purpose of heart, and I shall heal them; and ye shall be the means of bringing salvation unto them."[30] Opportunities to bring salvation to others will not end with your full-time mission, but continue throughout your life.

THE SAVIOR'S INVITATION—
CONTINUE TO BE HIS SERVANT

While you were on your mission, you experienced what it was like to live in a spiritual oasis. You obtained the word of God, asked for the Lord's help and direction, sought missionary experiences, invited others to come unto Christ, and saved the lives of others and yourself. These are not new concepts to you. You simply need to continue applying them in your life after the mission. As you do so, you will continue to be a servant of the Lord and you will keep your spiritual glow. With the prophet Mormon, you will be able to say throughout the rest of your life, "I am a disciple of Jesus Christ, the Son of God. I have been called of him to declare his word among his people, that they might have everlasting life."[31]

Remember Nephi's vision. He saw a spiritual oasis in which there was a beautiful tree. An angel was teaching Nephi what his vision meant and he "beheld that the tree of life was a representation of the love of God.

And the angel said unto [him] again: Look and behold the condescension of God! And [he] looked and beheld the Redeemer of the world."[32]

Jesus Christ embodies the love we should feel for others. His invitations of love are to all mankind:

- "Come unto me all ye ends of the earth, buy milk and honey, without money and without price."[33]

- "Repent, all ye ends of the earth, and come unto me and be baptized in my name, that ye may be sanctified by the reception of the Holy Ghost, that ye may stand spotless before me at the last day."[34]

- "Come unto me, all ye that labour and are heavy laden, and I will give you rest."[35]

We are the messengers who must deliver these invitations. We must continue to invite others and ourselves to "come unto Christ, and be perfected in him."[36]

Suggestions for Parents

The most difficult thing for both of my children who served missions was to lose the mantle of being a missionary. They handled it in different ways but they felt so alone in comparison to how they felt on their mission, which was surrounded by the gospel and surrounded by the Spirit. As they started to have experiences in the real world every day, it was tough for them to hold on to the Spirit. One of my children, in the first week she was home, just crashed. Crashed and burned. Breaking her heart and my heart, too.

       ▸ MOTHER OF A RETURNED MISSIONARY

Returned missionaries have become new creatures in Christ. In order to maintain that new creature status, they must continue in their eternal purpose and "live . . . no more after the flesh."[37] That is hard to do! As families and friends, we need to support our returned missionaries in their righteousness and make sure their lives and our lives continue in accordance with our eternal purpose.

LEARN FROM YOUR RETURNED MISSIONARY

As a mother, I have loved to see my missionaries leave home as youngsters in the gospel who are still dependent on me for direction, and return as independent adults who are able to stand on their own light and knowledge. I have been able to learn from them and enjoy their newfound maturity in the gospel. My missionaries have shared with me many choice and meaningful insights that have strengthened my testimony of the gospel.

I had a gospel discussion with my recently returned missionary son, William, who shared with me his understanding of the oft-used missionary verses, Moroni 10:4–5. These verses state that the Holy Ghost will help us know and feel that something is true for "he will manifest the truth of it unto [us]."[38] William pointed out to me that the Holy Ghost's role to manifest truth is different from his role of facilitating our knowledge of all things. People can know that something is true without understanding everything about it.

Many converts on his mission (and members, too) misunderstood this scripture and thought the Holy Ghost would help them understand and know everything about the gospel, so that they would never have any doubts about anything ever again. The Holy Ghost testifies of truth, but a sure knowledge often comes much later after hard work and effort, albeit still through the Holy Ghost. Sometimes, that knowledge is not acquired in this life, but in the life hereafter. I listened to his insight and marveled. Our roles had changed, as I became the student and he the teacher.

ENCOURAGE YOUR RETURNED MISSIONARY AS A GOSPEL SCHOLAR

What a great blessing it is in a returned missionary's life (and your family's life as well) when you, as a parent, encourage your returned missionary to continue along this path of spiritual independence! You may need to ask questions and give them confidence in their new role as scripture teacher and scholar in your home. Sometimes, they may look to you to make sure this is all right. They want to make sure that they are not doing anything that would offend you or upset the balance of authority in your home. As you encourage them to share their insights and praise them for the depth of their understanding, they will become increasingly comfortable in doing so, creating a stronger bond between their experiences of sharing the gospel on their mission and their post-mission life.

Returned missionaries need to continue to have teaching experiences to keep their testimonies bright. You may want to consider some of the following ideas to provide opportunities for such experiences:

- Invite them to teach family home evening lessons to your family on different gospel topics, such as how to do missionary work, how to incorporate the Atonement in your life, and how to teach gospel principles.

- Host a fireside with neighbors, friends, and people in your ward where they can relate the experiences they had on the mission. This can also be a missionary opportunity for those outside our faith to understand what missionaries do on a mission.

- Invite them to work with the ward mission leader and full-time missionaries in your ward and stake. Encourage them to go out regularly with the missionaries so they can continue to have missionary experiences.

- Encourage and enable them to invite friends over to your home, especially those friends who may be interested in learning more about the gospel. Help them become active member missionaries.

BE A MISSIONARY YOURSELF

Recently, Steve went to a conference in Europe for his work. Inspired by his interactions with our recently returned missionary son as well as with other older children who had served missions, he prepared for an opportunity to talk to some of his colleagues about the gospel if the opportunity came up during his trip.

As he prayed, he felt he should take along a Book of Mormon, and because the conference was in France, he went to Deseret Book and picked up a Book of Mormon in French as well. He told the Lord in his prayers, "I'm preparing and trying to do my part. Please lead me to someone."

At the conference, he was sitting at a dinner banquet discussing his family, his work, and his church. The woman next to him leaned over and asked, "How is your church different from the other churches?" Don't you just love it when people ask those kinds of questions? Because of his own missionary training, he was able to give her a five-minute version of the first discussion, including telling her about the Book of Mormon. However, she was Italian, not French! As it turned out, the only other Mormon at the conference was his friend, who had gone to church in France the previous Sunday, knew where the local ward was, and knew who to call to try to find an Italian Book of Mormon. After several phone calls, including one to the local mission office, two missionaries delivered an Italian Book of Mormon to him at the conference the next day—the last afternoon of the conference. When he presented the Italian Book of Mormon to the woman, she thanked him profusely and asked, "How did you ever get an Italian version of this book?" He replied, "It was a small miracle, but I believe that God wanted you to have it."

Whether you have been a full-time missionary previously or not, you, as a parent, can be an example of missionary work. You can pray and seek inspiration for missionary experiences at home, at work, or just walking down the street. These actions will inspire your returned missionaries to continue sharing the gospel the same way they inspired you while on their mission. You may even want to ask them for ideas, assistance, and suggestions for furthering your own missionary efforts. Missionary work should be a family affair, and inviting your returned missionaries to help will strengthen both them and you as you engage in this great work together.

SAVE YOUR RETURNED MISSIONARY

Unfortunately, some missionaries may become less active or even leave the Church after returning home. They may question their testimonies and whether what they did as a missionary was of any real value. As a parent, you may become discouraged as you struggle with how to help them rebuild their faith. They are adults and need to have the freedom to choose their paths, and yet, we still have an eternal stewardship over them as their parents.

Alma the Younger did not believe in the Church of Jesus Christ anymore, even though his father Alma was a prophet. While on his way to persecute members of the Church, an angel appeared to him and said: "Behold, the Lord hath heard the prayers of . . . his servant, Alma, who is thy father; for he has prayed with much faith concerning thee that thou mightiest be brought to the knowledge of the truth; therefore, for this purpose have I come to convince thee of the power and authority of God, that the prayers of his servants might be answered according to their faith."[39]

Your returned missionary will probably not be as unrighteous as Alma the Younger in "seeking to destroy the church,"[40] but your prayers will most certainly be heard with the same concern and love as Alma's father's prayers were heard. Remember, your returned missionary was the Lord's full-time servant and He loves him or her very much. Of course, your prayers will probably not be answered by an angel. Instead, the answer may come in the form of a home teacher, visiting teacher, friend, former companion, or concerned priesthood leader.

The scripture cited earlier in this chapter also applies to these returned missionaries: "Unto such shall ye continue to minister; for ye know not but what they will return and repent, and come unto me with full purpose of heart, and I shall heal them; and ye shall be the means of bringing salvation unto them."[41]

One returned sister missionary recently wrote us about a former companion who had become less active after returning home. In the letter, she said that she and other sisters who had known this less-active sister on the mission began to reach out and fellowship her. The bond between those who have served the Lord together is a very powerful one! Daily contacts via social media became the vehicle by which this sister was finally strengthened and helped back to activity. She has recently been called as a Relief Society teacher in her ward. All who reached out to her rejoiced greatly with her return, and we did, too! All of us felt to exclaim as did Alma: "Behold, when I see [my sister] truly penitent, and coming to the Lord [her] God, then is my soul filled with joy; then do I remember what the Lord has done, . . . even that he hath heard my prayer."[42]

RE-EVALUATE YOUR HOME ENVIRONMENT

We often ask the returned missionaries in our institute class: When you returned home, how many of you felt that your family could improve in their family prayers, family scripture study, and family home evenings? Usually, almost every hand goes up! We can all do better in these areas. As you prepare for the return of your missionary, re-evaluate the frequency and quality of these essential family activities. Involve all family members, even the youngest children, in counseling together to identify and then implement ideas for improvement. The following are some questions you may wish to ask yourselves:

- Is our home a spiritual oasis from the world?

- How can we improve our family prayers, scripture study, and home evenings?

- What can we do to increase our family missionary and temple experiences together?

- Are there movies, books, magazines, video games, or other media in our home that might make our returned missionary feel uncomfortable and that we should remove to better follow the standards in *For the Strength of Youth*?

Use the answers to these questions to direct your actions in preparing for your missionary's return. As you do so, you will be ready to meet their glowing countenance with an increased glow of your own!

NOTES

1. 2 Corinthians 5:16, footnote a; from Joseph Smith Translation. 2 Corinthians 5:17.
2. Exodus 34:29.
3. Exodus 34:30.
4. Exodus 34:33.
5. Matthew 5:16.
6. Marianne Holman Prescott, "Returned Missionaries Need a Friend, a Responsibility, and Spiritual Nourishment," *Church News*, February 18, 2014.
7. James 1:27.
8. James 1:27, footnote g; from Joseph Smith Translation.
9. Doctrine and Covenants 59:9.
10. 1 Nephi 8:27.
11. See Moroni 7:16–17.
12. Doctrine and Covenants 123:12.
13. See Neal A. Maxwell, *A Wonderful Flood of Light* (Salt Lake City, Utah: Bookcraft, 1990), 47.
14. Alma 32:42.
15. Doctrine and Covenants 11:21.
16. Doctrine and Covenants 84:85.
17. *Preach My Gospel* (Salt Lake City, Utah: The Church of Jesus Christ of Latter-day Saints, 2004), 17.
18. Julie B. Beck, "My Soul Delighteth in the Scriptures," *Ensign*, May 2004.
19. *Preach My Gospel*, 22–24.
20. Matthew 21:22. See also 3 Nephi 18:20–21 and Moroni 7:26.
21. Cyrus H. Wheelock, "Ye Elders of Israel," *Hymnal*, (Salt Lake City, Utah: The Church of Jesus Christ of Latter-day Saints), 319.
22. 2 Corinthians 3:3.
23. Sarah Jane Weaver, "Share more gospel messages on social media, Elder Bednar says," *Church News*, August 19, 2014.

24. M. Russell Ballard, "Put Your Trust in the Lord," *Ensign,* November 2013.
25. Doctrine and Covenants 20:59.
26. Alma 5:33–34.
27. *Preach My Gospel,* 170.
28. Doctrine and Covenants 18:15.
29. See Doctrine and Covenants 4:4.
30. 3 Nephi 18:32
31. 3 Nephi 5:13.
32. 1 Nephi 11:25–27.
33. 2 Nephi 26:25.
34. 3 Nephi 27:20.
35. Matthew 11:28.
36. Moroni 10:32.
37. 2 Corinthians 5:16, footnote a; from Joseph Smith Translation.
38. Moroni 10:4.
39. Mosiah 27:14.
40. Mosiah 27:10.
41. 3 Nephi 18:32.
42. Alma 29:10.

You can never say Preach My Gospel *doesn't apply to me anymore. I should read it more often now that I'm home.*

> RETURNED MISSIONARY ELDER

I read Preach My Gospel *when I got back from my mission because it spoke in a language I could understand. It made me feel comfortable, like I was back on my mission.*

> RETURNED MISSIONARY ELDER

Using *Preach My Gospel* Forever

DON'T THROW EVERYTHING AWAY

Coming home, you may feel like you need to get rid of all your missionary stuff and replace it with items that will help you fit into your new life. You should absolutely throw away your shoes with holes in the toe and loose soles that flap every time you take a step. You elders probably have many "white" shirts that are now a dingy yellow and will never return to that crisp pre-mission whiteness. Those shirts can probably be thrown away, too. You don't need to wear a white shirt and tie every day now, but you should definitely pick up a couple of new white shirts so that you can look like a returned missionary when you go to church. You sisters will probably want to get rid of the black skirt you wore almost every day on your mission. You may also want to throw away some of your dresses that are now threadbare and full of holes. You don't need to wear a skirt every day now, but you should be dressed modestly so that you are still an example to others as a returned missionary. Obviously, you should not throw away other items you brought home from your mission. These include your carefully marked scriptures, notes, memories from your mission (hopefully recorded in your journal), the addresses of your converts, and the pictures you took. And never throw away the spiritual growth you gained on your mission, your understanding of the doctrines found in the Book of Mormon, or your increased testimony of the gospel of Jesus Christ.

PREACH MY GOSPEL

Another item that you should definitely keep forever is your copy of *Preach My Gospel*. Whether you have one in English or in another language, this book has been a dear friend and a source of guidance and inspiration during your mission. You read it, studied it, and learned from its pages for eighteen months or two years. You studied it with your companions—sometimes as long as two to three hours a day when you were being trained or training another missionary.

If you've been home from your mission for a while, perhaps you've already put your copy of *Preach My Gospel* away somewhere, thinking that you don't need it anymore. Nothing could be further from the truth! As time goes on after your return, you may begin to feel that something is missing in your life, even though you are still reading your scriptures every day. Go and find your *Preach My Gospel*, pull it out, open it up, and as you begin to read it again, ask yourself, "How can I apply this to my life now as a returned missionary?" If you ask that question with real intent, and even prayerfully, new vistas of understanding will open to your view and the Spirit will begin to teach you, just as it did on your mission, how to use this wonderful manual now.

You will find that each chapter of *Preach My Gospel* contains essential guidance for your post-mission life. Here are some examples:

- You can rediscover your continuing purpose as a Latter-day Saint who professes to believe in and strives to live the doctrine of Christ (Chapter 1).

- You can continue to improve the effectiveness of your daily scripture study and learn how to liken the teachings of the scriptures to the situations of your life now (Chapter 2).

- You can find new insights as well as strengthen your existing knowledge of the basic doctrines and principles of the gospel, and you can continue to refine your ability to teach them to your family and friends (Chapter 3).

- More than ever before in your life, including during your mission, you need to recognize and understand the Spirit as you make decisions that will affect the rest of your life and eternity (Chapter 4).

- You can continue to focus your study on the Book of Mormon and constantly remind yourself why it always needs to be the cornerstone of your testimony (Chapter 5).

- You can continue to develop and to assess your progress regarding Christlike attributes, which is definitely a life-long pursuit (Chapter 6).

- Even if you didn't learn a language on your mission, you can open new opportunities professionally and in your church service by learning one now, and those who learned a language will always be benefitted by retaining that ability (Chapter 7).

- With the demands of school, work, church, and social expectations, keeping yourself organized and setting goals is essential to your success as a returned missionary (Chapter 8).

- You can improve your people skills and continue to find and invite people to come unto Christ by using the finding techniques you developed on your mission. These same techniques can be used to help you find an eternal companion as well (Chapter 9).

- You will continue to teach people throughout your life, whether in your church calling, as a parent, or in your profession. You will also most certainly have the opportunity to help others (and yourself) to overcome bad habits and behaviors throughout your life (Chapter 10).

- You can always strengthen your resolve to keep the commitments and covenants you have made and teach and help others to do the same (Chapter 11).

- Throughout your life, you will have opportunities to help prepare others for baptism, whether they are your own children, your grandchildren, or others (Chapter 12).

- As a returned missionary, you now have the opportunity to be the kind of missionary-minded ward member you always loved to work with on your mission and to help your ward and stake leaders hasten the missionary work in your area (Chapter 13).

Preach My Gospel is referred to and quoted throughout this book because of the eternal principles it teaches. Again, please don't throw it away or hide it under your bed. If you learn anything from reading this book, it should be that continuing to study and follow the teachings contained in *Preach My Gospel* is a key to your successful transition to post-mission life.

Suggestions for Parents

What a surprise it would be for your missionaries to return home to discover that you know and love *Preach My Gospel* as much as they do! Get your own copy of *Preach My Gospel* and start to read it individually and as a family. You will better understand what your missionaries have been doing during their time away from home as well as how you can help them in their transition to life after the mission.

When *Preach My Gospel* was first released to members of the Church, we decided that we would read *Preach My Gospel* as a family for our scripture study that year. We enjoyed every page! We learned how to internalize gospel principles, how to become better Latter-day Saints, and how to improve our family missionary efforts.

Elder M. Russell Ballard extended this same invitation to all members of the church: "I invite all members, regardless of your current calling or level of activity in the Church, to obtain a copy of *Preach My Gospel*. It is available through our distribution centers and also online. The online version can be read or downloaded at no cost. It is a guidebook for missionary work—which means it is a guidebook for all of us. Read it, study it, and then apply what you learn"[1]

Elder Ballard also encouraged parents and family members of missionaries to study *Preach My Gospel* and to share their insights with their missionaries: "You can tell the missionaries that you are studying *Preach My Gospel* and ask them to show you what they are learning in their studies. . . . Can you imagine the impact if family and friends included things they are learning from their personal study of *Preach My Gospel* in their letters and emails to their full-time missionaries?"[2]

FOLLOWING UP

After your missionary returns home, continue to follow up with them about their reading of *Preach My Gospel*. They used the principle of follow-up extensively with their investigators on their mission and they also became very accustomed to having their mission leaders and president follow up with them on their own goals and commitments. This eternal principle is taught beautifully in Chapter 11 of *Preach My Gospel*: "Extending an invitation without following up is like beginning a journey without finishing it or buying a ticket to a concert without going into the theater. Without the completed action, the commitment is hollow."[3] Don't get too busy with life that you forget to follow up with your returned missionary, especially on their continuing study of *Preach My Gospel* and the scriptures. Following up will strengthen the habits that they developed on their mission. These habits are essential to a lifetime of dedicated activity and service in the Church.

Become intimately familiar with *Preach My Gospel* yourself so that you can discuss some of its inspired and profound teachings together. This will enable your returned missionary to feel more comfortable during their transition, since they are used to having a companion with whom they can discuss spiritual insights and feelings. Reading and studying *Preach My Gospel* together will enable both you and your missionary to understand your eternal purpose better and to more faithfully live the doctrine of Christ as His devoted disciples.

NOTES

1. M. Russell Ballard, "Following Up," *Ensign, May* 2014.

2. Ibid.

3. *Preach My Gospel* (Salt Lake City, Utah: The Church of Jesus Christ of Latter-day Saints, 2004), 200.

Coming back was definitely interesting. I did not expect it to be what it was. My dad is currently in Afghanistan and he was able to come home when I came home. So, he was there and to have both my parents there was really great. Just having the support of both of your parents and knowing that they are there for you is something that I would not trade for the world. I know no matter what I do or how much I screw up, my parents will always be there for me.

‣ RETURNED MISSIONARY SISTER

One of the challenges I faced coming home was the different dynamics in my family. Toward the end of my mission, my uncle was actually killed in a plane crash. Coming home, I definitely saw the effects it had on my family—their beliefs and their faith. Some of my cousins that joined the Church before I left on my mission now say that they don't believe in the Church anymore. That has been really hard for me. I still want to have that missionary spirit. I try to encourage them and to really show them how much the gospel is true and how much happiness it can bring us.

‣ RETURNED MISSIONARY SISTER

Well, out of all of the challenges I faced coming home, I guess the biggest one was family life. It was definitely different. My grandparents had moved in with us. I had been on my mission for three months when I found this out via email. My grandpa wasn't doing so well. He was really sick, actually. That was probably the hardest thing—coming home and seeing the changes that have happened to my family and the toll it has taken.

‣ RETURNED MISSIONARY ELDER

Dealing with Family Changes

FAMILY CHANGES

Many things can happen during the time you were gone from home. You can come home to a new house, a new community, new brothers- or sisters-in-law, new nieces or nephews, or even new brothers or sisters.

Two of our children were serving their missions when we were called to serve in Brazil. Both of them had grown up in the Northwest. All of their friends lived in Redmond, Washington, yet they came home to Brazil without knowing Portuguese or anyone there, except our family. Another son was called on his mission while we lived in Brazil. While he served his mission, we decided to relocate to Utah. He returned from his mission to a new home, new ward, and new community. We personally witnessed how difficult it was for these valiant missionaries to come home to such extreme changes.

Some returned missionaries have to deal with the death of a loved one while they are on their mission. We had missionaries in our mission who experienced the sudden death of a parent, grandparent, aunt, uncle, or sibling while they were serving. Once, during lunch at a zone conference, we received a call from the mother of one of our zone leaders who said that his father had suddenly passed away. His father had not been sick and there had been no warning. He had just died very suddenly. It was so difficult for this wonderful elder, but his spiritual strength sustained him when he was told what had happened. He talked to his mother and his brothers and sisters, but he did not want it to affect his work. He knew that his dad would have wanted it that way. He did not return home to go to the funeral. Instead, he immersed himself in his work.

Another missionary had to deal with the death of his mother. He wrote to his president later: "I will never forget when you told me that my mom had passed away. Immediately afterward, you put your arms around me and just held me for a few minutes. And you know the lamb that Jesus is holding in the picture in the front of the Restoration pamphlet? Yes, that's about how I felt. Of course, I didn't realize until afterward that I felt like that, nor that that was exactly what I needed in that moment. But, it was perfect . . . The private outpouring of love that you . . . gave me during that difficult time in my mission was an essential part of my getting through that obstacle."[1]

These missionaries were full of the Spirit during their missions. They were supported by the Spirit in a very real way as they continued forward, even after such tragedies. They had faith in the doctrine of Christ and in the plan of salvation, which they were teaching to others. They understood the promises of the resurrection and the Atonement, which buoyed them up and kept them going during these hard times.

If you had to deal with the loss of someone you loved during the mission, you may not have felt the full reality of their loss until you returned home and found they were not there. You may need to go through the grieving process again, even though a significant amount of time has passed. Allow yourself time to grieve. If you need some additional support to go through this emotional time, seek counsel from your family, priesthood leaders, or even a professional counselor as you deal with these very real and difficult emotions.

SPIRITUAL CHANGES

Spiritual changes of both a positive and negative nature can happen at home during the time you are on your mission. Other friends, siblings, and grandparents may have left on missions and may not be home when you arrive. You will miss them and perhaps feel sad that you missed attending their farewells and hearing about their missionary experiences while you were gone.

Your family may have become better about holding family scripture study, family prayer, and family home evening, and with their individual study and prayers as well. On the other hand, your family may have become lax about going to church or about prayers and scripture reading.

One of our Brazilian elders joined the Church on his own at the age of eighteen, the only member of his family to be baptized. Two months later, he baptized his younger brother, but his parents were still skeptical about the Church. When he left on his mission a year later, he did not have the support of his parents. They did not even come to the airport to say goodbye and his father thought he would be wasting his time for two years. He still wrote his family every week bearing his testimony of the gospel and the great work he was doing. The members of his home ward reached out to his family, lovingly becoming their friends and inviting them to Church.

After being on his mission for only two months, his mother was baptized, and three months after that, a real miracle happened when his father was baptized. His father had completely changed in his attitude about the gospel. While this elder was still on his mission, his parents traveled to the temple in Campinas, Brazil, and he was able to join them there as they received their endowment. They were then sealed together as a family for time and for all eternity. That sacred event changed his family dramatically and he felt a tremendous difference in his home when he returned after his mission.

Another dear sister came home to a very different change in her family. Her family had been new converts to the Church. When she left on her mission, they were very active and supportive of her going on a mission. While she was away, a cousin had died because of a tragic accident. They could not understand how the Lord could allow this to happen to such a beloved member of their family. This became a major trial of their faith and her family decided to leave the Church. She returned home to a family that was very negative about her faith and did not want to hear anything about her missionary experiences. Coming home, she felt very isolated and alone as the only member of her family who was still active in the Church.

DON'T HOLD BACK

These examples represent the two extremes of spiritual change you may face when you come home. However, most returned missionaries feel that their homes are spiritually different in some way or another when they return. As we have talked to returned missionaries who come to our institute class, we have been struck by the consistency of their comments about how different everything feels. They have said that their family feels different. Their life feels different. Their relationships with their friends feel different. Their goals feel different. The direction they want their life to follow is often different, too.

You came home on a spiritual high after a period of accelerated spiritual growth during your mission. You studied the gospel and served the Lord twenty-four hours a day, seven days a week. As you come home, you must maintain that same focus. If your purpose is truly the same, then your commitment to the Lord should be the same as well.

One sister missionary searched for a mantra to keep her focused on serving the Lord both during and after her mission. She picked the words of Paul found in the Book of Acts. Paul was visiting with his fellow saints in Ephesus while traveling back home to Jerusalem. He reminded these dearly beloved saints about his ministry and his many deeds of service to them: "Ye know, from the first day that I came into Asia, after what manner I have been with you at all seasons, serving the Lord with all humility of mind, and with many tears . . . and how *I kept back nothing* . . . and have taught you publickly, and from house to house."[2] The phrase "I kept back nothing" became the focus for her life. She would give her all in everything she did on her mission, and she would keep nothing back from the Lord when she came home as well.

Continuing to "keep back nothing" may be more difficult given the situation in your family, with your friends, at your work, or in the world around you. But you can do it! You can still be a servant of the Lord. Do not let these changes cause you to lose your focus. You now have the opportunity as well as the responsibility to help your family, friends, and others learn and grow in the gospel, just as your helped your investigators.

Suggestions for Parents

All family changes will affect your returned missionary. Sometimes, you, as a parent, forget everything that has happened while your children were gone. It's difficult to express everything in letters to your missionary. Some things are better left unsaid, too. You do not want to worry them unnecessarily while they are away. But, now that they are home, they will need to deal with these various new situations.

The following chart is a tool you can use to fill out. It will focus your thoughts on what changes have happened to your family while your missionary has been gone. This chart will help jog your memory and real-ize that your son or daughter will be coming home to changes.

FAMILY CHANGES

Major family events, esp. events to celebrate	New people who are important to our family	Emotional challenges our family has faced	Physical challenges our family has faced	Spiritual challenges our family has faced

After you have written down these changes, you will be better pre-pared to support your missionary in the new and different family atmo-sphere they may encounter at home.

ALLOW YOUR MISSIONARY TIME TO GRIEVE

As mentioned before, if someone in your family or a close family friend has passed away while your missionary was serving, the full reality of grief may not happen until they return home. Even though a signifi-cant amount of time may have passed, they have been putting off these emotions while serving the Lord. Now, the full force of their grief may overwhelm them.

Sometimes, watching your returned missionary go through this may be difficult for the rest of the family because they have already dealt with their grief and moved on with their lives. Realize that your family and your returned missionary may need some additional support from other relatives, priesthood leaders, and perhaps even professional counselors as they deal with these real and raw emotions once again.

SPIRITUAL CHANGES

Often, you, as a parent, will not have had the time or opportunity to progress at the same spiritual rate as your missionary while they have been away. Your children at home may not have had the time or the inclination for such spiritual growth either. The same may be true for your returned missionary's friends. But you do not want your missionary's spiritual trajectory to be lowered upon returning home.

Parents and family members can and should strive to rise up and join their missionaries in their spiritual climb upward. You can do it! A missionary's return home is the perfect opportunity to evaluate and improve the spiritual atmosphere in your home. You can increase your study of the scriptures as a family and as individuals, and have regular family and personal prayers and a weekly family home evening if you are not already doing these things. Your home will thus become a place where your missionary will feel spiritually comfortable pursuing their eternal purpose. Your missionary has strived to keep back nothing from the Lord and this should be your goal as well.

BECOME THE KIND OF ADULT
YOU WANT THEM TO BECOME

As a parent, you are extremely busy. You need to ask yourself if you are busy doing the things that matter most. Your returned missionary will be looking to you as an example. Are you the kind of adult you want them to be? Are you doing what you expect them to do as a returned missionary? If not, perhaps you must repent. Your Heavenly Father loves both you and your returned missionary, and because of His love, He can and will enable you to change through the power of the Atonement of His Son. Your missionary taught this principle for eighteen months or two years. It is true!

All of us need to practice repentance every day. We are all battling against the natural man tendencies of the world that are constantly working against us. If we do not fight against those tendencies, subtle changes may enter into our hearts and our actions without us even noticing. King Benjamin describes the natural man as "an enemy to God . . . unless he yields to the enticings of the Holy Spirit, and putteth off the natural man and becometh a saint through the atonement of Christ the Lord, and becometh as a child."[3]

BECOMING THE CHILD

Consider your returned missionary a blessing from God to help you continue to overcome the natural man and to improve! This is possible if you are willing to exchange the roles you had before their mission. Let them become the teacher, the parent, and you the student, the child. The humility this requires will strengthen your abilities to feel the Spirit. The Lord can work through our returned missionaries, if we let Him. As we become as a child, we also take upon ourselves the qualities of meekness, humility, patience, love, and submission. We will be willing "to submit to all things which the Lord seeth fit to inflict upon [us], even as a child doth submit to his father."[4] This switching of roles can help us learn and grow together with our spiritually matured returned missionaries.

NOTES

1. Personal letter.
2. Acts 20:18–20; emphasis added.
3. Mosiah 3:19.
4. Ibid.

Coming home from a mission, I and probably most, if not all other missionaries, felt like we had new talents with how to accomplish goals and how we viewed life, and we had a lot of confidence in ourselves in how we can accomplish and do things. But, I felt that going home, people did not see that. It was hard to deal with that. You know what you are capable of, but these people haven't been around you for two years, so they really don't know.

➤ RETURNED MISSIONARY ELDER

My first week back was really hard. I thought I knew what I wanted to do. I thought I wanted to sell security systems or work at the MTC, but neither of those things worked out like I wanted them to. So I just prayed a lot. I finally found some really great jobs that I'm really loving now. I learned that if we continue with faith, God will bless us. As returned missionaries, He will guide us where He wants us to be. I feel like He has really led me to do the things I have done so far.

➤ RETURNED MISSIONARY ELDER

Rising above Challenges

When you first entered your mission, you probably felt overwhelmed. You may have also felt lost and questioned what you were doing on a mission because the reality of the experience was so different from what you had expected. Yet those feelings changed once you started accomplishing what you were supposed to do—what you felt the Lord wanted you to do.

One sister wrote in her final missionary letter, "I don't even have words to describe what I feel. This past year and a half has passed more quickly than I could have imagined. It has also been more rewarding than I could have imagined. . . . The miracles and heartaches and memories are marked in me forever."[1]

The same is true with this new journey of post-mission life. You may experience feelings of self-doubt, confusion, and sometimes frustration. We have asked the returned missionaries we teach: "What are the top two or three challenges or difficulties you have faced since returning home?" Their responses have varied greatly, but we have observed many common ones:

- Dealing with the death of a loved one,
- Deciding how to handle friends who have such different values from mine,
- Figuring out what to study at school,

- Finding a job,
- Making enough money to pay for an apartment,
- Having money for food,
- Paying for a car,
- Going on dates, and
- Generally feeling lost.

The mountains you have to climb, figuratively, may seem insurmountable. President Eyring reminded us: "If the foundation of faith is not embedded in our hearts, the power to endure will crumble. . . . If we have faith in Jesus Christ, the hardest as well as the easiest times in life can be a blessing."[2] With time, your feelings will change. Your confidence in yourself and in your ability to deal with your new life will increase with the Lord's help. President Eyring continued, "We never need to feel that we are alone or unloved in the Lord's service because we never are. . . . The Lord watches over you. God the Father lives. His Beloved Son, Jesus Christ, is our Redeemer. His love is unfailing."[3] Just as you relied on the love and care of the Lord during your mission, you can rely upon His love now.

FEELING THE SPIRIT OF THE LORD IN YOUR LIFE NOW!

Think about your time as a missionary and ask yourself:

- How often did I pray every day?
- How many hours a day did I read the scriptures?
- How close did I feel to the Spirit of the Lord?

A companionship of sisters in our mission decided that they would count how many prayers they said in a day. They prayed before and after personal and companion study, they prayed before they walked into a home, they prayed before and after they taught, they prayed over meals, and they prayed to thank Heavenly Father for His Spirit after they left each lesson. They stopped counting the number of prayers they said that day when they reached twenty-five, and they visited more homes and prayed many more times after that.

Now that you are home, how often do you pray? Do you sometimes feel like your prayers don't make it through the ceiling? As a missionary, you taught from Lesson 4 of *Preach My Gospel*: "As we pray with faith, sincerity, and real intent, we will see God's influence in our lives. He will guide us in our daily lives and help us make good decisions."[4]

While you may not be able to pray as many times each day as you did on your mission, almost every returned missionary we've spoken to who has increased the number and quality of their prayers throughout the day has experienced a marked and corresponding increase in feeling the Spirit, often returning to or even surpassing the level of spirituality they felt on their mission. One returned sister missionary came up with the idea of setting a reminder on her smartphone that would go off each hour, reminding her to offer a silent prayer no matter where she was or what she was doing. She later remarked that this one thing had brought her closer to the Spirit than ever before.

Another returned sister missionary asked, "Why don't I feel the same closeness with the Lord now that I am home? I constantly felt the Spirit while I was on my mission. The Spirit would direct me on which doors to knock and which people to contact. I constantly felt his direction in my life as a missionary. Now, I feel like the Lord does not tell me anything and I am floundering!"

After discussing her feelings, we came up with two reasons why the Lord did not seem to be directing her life in the same way. First, she was not praying nor was she reading her scriptures as often during the day. Second, we observed that the Lord may want her to start making some of her decisions on her own. She needed to make a decision based on the facts, her feelings, and advice from parents and other trusted advisors. Then, she needed to take it to the Lord rather than always asking the Lord to tell her what to do without putting thought and effort into the decision first.

Jesus Christ taught his disciples while he was still with them, "But the Comforter, which is the Holy Ghost, whom the Father will send in my name, he shall teach you all things, and bring all things to your remembrance, whatsoever I have said unto you."[5] The prophet Nephi also taught about the power of the Holy Ghost: "If ye will enter in by the way, and receive the Holy Ghost, it will show unto you all things what ye should do."[6]

You probably used these scriptures many times on your mission, testifying to your investigators that the Holy Ghost would teach them what to do, if they did their part. As you now make the most important decisions in your life, you must apply this same principle! You must receive the Holy Ghost, follow the commandments, and have a desire that coincides with the desires of the Lord. You must match your will to His.

In Section 11 of the Doctrine and Covenants, the word "desire" is used eight times by the Lord. The Lord is teaching Hyrum Smith how his righteous desires will work together with his faith in the Lord. The Lord mentions at the end of this section that He is talking to "all who have good desires,"[7] and not just to Hyrum.

In His instruction to Hyrum and to us, the Lord declares, "Verily, verily, I say unto you, I will impart unto you of my Spirit, which shall enlighten your mind, which shall fill your soul with joy; And then shall ye know, or by this shall you know, all things whatsoever you desire of me, which are pertaining unto things of righteousness, in faith believing in me that you shall receive."[8] Hyrum is also told that he would need to be patient and continue to "cleave unto [the Lord] with all [his] heart"[9] before he would receive his heart's desires.

WORKING FOR THE SPIRIT

Oliver Cowdery had a desire, but he was having a difficult time hearing and understanding the Holy Ghost. He had a similar problem to that of the young sister mentioned earlier. He wanted to translate the plates like Joseph Smith, but he needed the spirit of revelation to do it. He found the work of translation almost impossible and he was struggling. Finally, the Lord told Oliver that the privilege to translate was being taken away from him. The Lord said, "Behold, you have not understood; you have supposed that I would give it unto you, when you took no thought save it was to ask me. . . . You must study it out in your mind; then you must ask me if it be right, and if it is right I will cause that your bosom shall burn within you; therefore, you shall feel that it is right."[10]

The Lord also reminded Oliver of other revelatory feelings the Spirit had given to him when he was seeking answers to his questions: "Behold, thou knowest that thou hast inquired of me and I did enlighten thy mind; and now I tell thee these things that thou mayest know that thou hast been enlightened by the Spirit of truth. . . . Did I not speak peace to your mind concerning the matter? What greater witness can you have than from God?"[11] Just like Oliver, you must learn to recognize the revelatory feelings you have that come from God.

More than at any other time in your life, you are making decisions that will affect the rest of your life and eternity. It is absolutely essential that you have the constant companionship of the Holy Ghost to guide you in these decisions. You will need revelation to help you decide what to study in school, where to live, whom to date, and most important of all, whom to marry. These are just a few of the myriad choices that have eternal consequences for you and your future family.

Like Oliver, if you only ask without putting forth the necessary effort, the Spirit cannot give you the answer you seek. Instead, you may be told to study the situation further and then come back and ask again. With all the demands of your new life, finding and taking the time to do your part may be more difficult, but you can do it! You learned how to do this as a missionary. The Lord loves you just as much now and is just as willing to give you answers to your prayers as He was on your mission.

Elder Richard G. Scott gave us a marvelous step-by-step process for obtaining revelation from God when he related his own search for answers:

> As each impression came, I carefully wrote it down. In the process, I was given precious truths that I greatly needed in order to be a more effective servant of the Lord. . . . Subsequently I prayed, reviewing with the Lord what I thought I had been taught by the Spirit. When a feeling of peace came, I thanked Him for the guidance given. I was then impressed to ask, "Was there yet more to be given?" I received further impressions, and the process of writing down the impressions, pondering, and praying for confirmation was repeated. Again I was prompted to ask, "Is there more I should know?" And there was. When that last, most sacred experience was concluded, I had received some of the most precious, specific, personal direction one could hope to obtain in this life. Had I not responded to the first impressions and recorded them, I would not have received the last, most precious guidance.[12]

The process of listening to the Spirit, writing down your thoughts and impressions, praying and reviewing your answers with the Lord, thanking Him for His guidance, and asking if there is anything more you need to know is an iterative process you should follow over and over in your life. As you do, the process will become easier and more natural—just like any process you learn and practice. Remember, too, that in order to enjoy the

Spirit of the Lord with you always, you must be worthy, cultivate your spirituality, and work to obtain those spiritual blessings.

THE CHALLENGE OF WASTING TIME

One of the great challenges of being home is finding the time to do those simple things, such as scripture reading, prayer, and temple attendance. Where does all your time go? You may want to try a simple activity and keep a time log of all the activities you do in a day and how long you spend on each activity. You may find there are some activities you need to do less frequently, or stop doing altogether.

Alyssa loved being able to spend time with her younger sisters who were still in high school now that she was home from her mission. They really liked to go on Pinterest and pin to their boards, especially for their future weddings. They would look all over the site for their dream wedding dress, cake, announcements, and colors, even though none of them were dating anybody seriously. This was just a fun girl activity they enjoyed doing together. Sarah soon realized that she was spending as many as four to five hours a day doing this, rather than spending the time to read scriptures, or to attend the temple. As she became more aware of her use of time, she began to control her Internet time and make sure she had time in her day for more important, spiritual pursuits.

Dan had never played many video games before his mission. School and sports had always kept him very busy and he never had the time for them. After returning from his mission, he had lots of free time while he was waiting to go to college. He was having problems finding a temporary job, so his friends invited him to play *World of Warcraft*. After only a week, he was already playing it for several hours a day. He felt he was getting to know people online and the game did make him think, so it must be sharpening his mental skills—at least that is what he told himself. Playing the game definitely made his days fly by until school started. In fact, he did little else but play the game. Now, he was in school and found the constant allure of *World of Warcraft* very difficult to avoid. He found himself missing classes so he could play the game, and he sometimes even missed church, especially if he had been playing all Saturday night.

The previous situation is a sad but true one for some returned missionaries. If you find yourself falling into this pattern of behavior, stop it now! Elder Kevin W. Pearson said, "Elders and sisters, you simply cannot return from your mission, do a swan dive back into Babylon, and spend endless hours scoring meaningless points on pointless video games without falling into a deep spiritual sleep. . . . If you lose the Spirit, you are lost. Don't be distracted and deceived."[13] Begin to fill your life with more wholesome activities. Find a job (even a temporary one if you're waiting to go back to school), give service to others in need, get involved in family history, attend the temple, do your home and visit teaching, contact and strengthen your mission converts and companions, etc. There is so much more you can do! A busy returned missionary is a happy returned missionary!

Time-wasting activities are purposefully very alluring and bring momentary pleasure. Some entertaining activities, in moderation, can bring enjoyment and fun into our lives. But, if you let them, they will take over your life and keep you away from doing activities that will strengthen you spiritually.

THE SIN OF PORNOGRAPHY

The Internet is everywhere and will be a part of what you do every day. You will probably use it both at work and at home in order to communicate with people or to find information. Most of the forms you will fill out for school or job applications will all be done online. You will communicate with your old companions and former investigators through social media. Out of necessity, you will probably be on the Internet a lot each day.

The Internet is a great tool that can help you be more organized and efficient. As already discussed, it can also be a big time waster. But, more than that, it can be a toxic tempter with lurid or suggestive pictures that pop up on your screen, even when you did not want them to. If you use YouTube or other public sites, advertisements will appear on the sides of your screen that will be there to titillate and tempt you to click. Realize that if you succumb to the temptation, you may find it very hard to stop. Pornography is terribly addicting and it will absolutely deaden your spirit.

Elder Richard G. Scott spoke emphatically about the destructive power of pornography, warning all members of the Church to beware of this pernicious challenge of the latter-days: "Satan has become a master at using the addictive power of pornography to limit individual capacity to be led by the Spirit. . . . This potent tool of Lucifer degrades the mind and the heart and the soul of any who use it. All who are caught in its seductive, tantalizing web and remain so will become addicted to its immoral, destructive influence."[14] Elder Pearson specifically warned returned missionaries that they could not "indulge in online pornography and ignore virtue and chastity without dire spiritual consequences."[15] Maintaining your virtue is a challenge that you absolutely must rise above and eliminate from your life. If you do fall into this trap, get help immediately from your priesthood leader. The longer you stay in the deadly quicksand of pornography, the harder it will be to get yourself out.

OVERCOMING BAD HABITS

You had to deal with the roadblock of addictive behaviors while teaching your investigators and preparing them for baptism. These behaviors would stop investigators in their progression forward and included such things as drugs, alcohol, coffee, smoking, pornography, and other forms of sexual immorality. You had the responsibility of teaching them how to change these behaviors that would otherwise be impossible to overcome without the power of the Atonement of Jesus Christ.

While you have hopefully not succumbed to one of these more serious problems, there will probably still be some habits in your life that may keep you from becoming the kind of individual you want to become. These "smaller sins" may include forgetting to read scriptures daily, not praying every morning, missing church, being negative toward others, or losing your temper too easily. You can use the same principles you taught your investigators in order to overcome your own bad habits.

As you know, these principles are outlined in Chapter 10 of *Preach My Gospel*:[16]

- Identify and acknowledge the problem through careful and honest self-examination.

- Acknowledge that the behavior is harmful, affects others, and requires change.

- Be humble and feel genuine sorrow.

- Seek forgiveness from others who have been harmed and learn to forgive yourself.

- Stop these bad actions and begin to do spiritually healthy things.

- Remain faithful to your covenants.

- Understand that the Lord will always love you, His child, even if you fall down again.

The same section of *Preach My Gospel* includes other practical suggestions that may help you in your quest to improve, such as making a plan for how you are going to stop a behavior, outlining what times, places, and people may be contributing to the behavior, writing down things you can do to avoid the behavior, seeking a priesthood blessing, and never giving up.[17] The Spirit will give you answers as you ask through prayer, with a sincere heart, for the Lord's help. And as you taught your investigators, you must be willing to change and exercise continual faith in the Lord Jesus Christ.

FOCUSING ON CHRISTLIKE ATTRIBUTES

Focusing on developing Christlike attributes is the best way to be rid of bad habits. "Christlike attributes are gifts from God. They come as you use your agency righteously. Ask your Heavenly Father to bless you with these attributes; you cannot develop them without His help. With a desire to please God, recognize your weaknesses and be willing and anxious to improve."[18] As you did on your mission, you can use the "Attribute Activity" on page 126 of *Preach My Gospel* to pinpoint areas you might like to focus on now that you are home. Often, problems you are facing can be resolved by changing yourself, rather than by trying to change others.

Andrew looked forward to coming home and reconnecting with his friends. A few of them had decided not to go on a mission but to stay and go to college to get a head start on their education. Andrew's best friend, Lance, was really excited to see him again. Initially, they both felt like their friendship was still strong. Then Lance began to make fun of Andrew. He would make fun of his missionary haircut, his weird clothes, and even the accent he had acquired from being a missionary in England. Andrew didn't know what to do. He did not want to stop being Lance's friend, yet the teasing wasn't funny anymore. Instead, it was becoming extremely annoying.

As Andrew pondered how to react, he remembered what he did when he was a new missionary with a trainer who turned out to be a very difficult companion. His trainer had decided that, because this was his last transfer, he was going to sleep in, enjoy the sights of the city, and not follow any of the mission rules. Andrew was frustrated and often very angry with his companion. One morning as he was praying about this problem, the thought came to him to look at Chapter 6 on Christlike attributes in *Preach My Gospel*. He took the Attribute Activity and then decided to work on patience. He read all the scriptures on patience he could and decided to change his attitude towards his companion. Andrew continued to live the mission rules, patiently waiting for his companion to change. It took time, but his companion did start to respond to Andrew's patient attitude. Finally, his companion started living the mission rules and they finished the transfer working hard together as obedient missionaries.

Andrew decided to try the same approach with Lance. He was patient with him and did not let his teasing cause him to get angry. He reread the scriptures on patience and prayed for the Lord's help for him to be strengthened in his love for and patience with Lance. The process took time, but he didn't lose his friend. Instead, Lance began to accept the changes Andrew had made in his life and these changes began to affect Lance for good, too. Lance started coming back to Church and asked Andrew sincerely about his mission and how he had converted others to the gospel. Andrew was grateful to see that Lance was beginning to feel the Spirit of conversion in his life as well. Andrew was also grateful for what he had learned on his mission about the power of Christlike attributes.

THREE THINGS YOU NEED AS A RETURNED MISSIONARY

President Gordon B. Hinckley gave strong counsel that every new convert needed three things: a friend, a church assignment, and to be "nourished by the good word of God."[19] As a missionary, you understood the importance of these principles in the lives of the people you baptized. Now that you are home, you also need to realize that you, as a returned missionary, need these three things in your life as well.

Marianne Prescott wrote in a Church News article, "Just like new converts making commitments to progress in the gospel, returning missionaries can apply the same principles they used with the people they taught on their mission as a guide when they return home and adjust to their new schedule."[20] You, as a returned missionary, need to find good friends, receive a calling in your ward, and continue to read and study the scriptures along with other spiritually nurturing activities.

FINDING GOOD FRIENDS

Some returned missionaries do not stay home very long. After a short time, they leave again for school or work, starting a new life away from home again. One elder said, "In some respects it was pretty wild because I didn't get to see my family hardly, and then I was right off, but I think in a lot of ways it was good, too. It felt like another transfer on my mission—going to a place I had never lived before in a new environment with new people. I think it was really good for me. It would have been pretty easy to kind of slip back two years if I were just hanging out at home with the same friends and environment."[21]

Other missionaries spend some time at home. This can also be a good experience, especially if you allow yourself to be a righteous example to your friends and family. The key is to constantly evaluate your situation and make whatever changes may be necessary.

You may find that the roommates in your new apartment do not live your standards. You may find that old friends are constantly trying to get you to do things you know are not in keeping with the way you want to live your life. No matter your situation, you may need to find new friends who have the same high standards that you do. The easiest way to find this kind of friend is at church on Sunday, at young single adult church activities, or at institute. If you consistently attend these meetings and activities, you will find young people who have the same standards you do and who are also looking for good friends like you. Former companions and missionaries from your mission may be another great source of friends with whom you can be equally yoked as you press onward and upward in your post-mission life.

SERVING IN THE CHURCH

You may want to attend a young single adult ward or your family's ward. You can make this decision with the help of your parents and priesthood leaders. Realize that it sometimes can take time to receive a calling. Consistently attend one ward so you become well known by your priesthood leaders and ward members, and your chances of receiving a calling quickly increase.

If you do not receive a calling promptly, ask the ward mission leader or the full-time missionaries for opportunities to teach with them. Ask your elders quorum president or your Relief Society president for a calling as a home or visiting teacher. You can also offer to visit less-active members and others in need of extra support in your ward. You do not need your leaders to come to you. Be the kind of proactive member you always hoped for and loved to have in the wards where you served on your mission. Always look for opportunities to be involved and serve.

NOURISHED BY THE GOOD WORD OF GOD

In the chapter on "Keeping the Glow," you were invited to continue always to obtain the word of God. In this chapter, we invite you to seek always to be nourished by the good word of God. Nourishment can include scripture study, church attendance, pondering, praying, and writing your spiritual thoughts and insights in a journal. One mission president told his returning missionaries: "You should study each day for a sufficient amount of time to have a revelatory experience. . . . It can be fifteen minutes or forty-five minutes. I try to plan sufficient time so the Spirit can reach me."[22]

Find time during your day to feast on the scriptures and "let the solemnities of eternity rest upon your minds."[23] You can assess your spiritual nourishment by tracking how long you spend reading scriptures and thinking about your Savior each day. You may need to be spiritually nourished at different times during the day, rather than taking a single hour-long block of time. You may only have time for short snacks throughout the day, rather than a long feast. For example, you may decide to spend some time in the morning, then a few minutes during your lunch hour, or a break at work, and then again, just before you go to bed.

You need to have a Plan A, Plan B, and Plan C for reading your scriptures, pondering, and praying, or it won't consistently happen. This is the same way you planned on your mission to make sure you accomplished the work. If you work at it, the Lord will help you figure out a way to fit the puzzle pieces of your schedule together effectively so that you can accomplish all that the Lord wants you to.

RISING ABOVE CHALLENGES

The challenges of coming home can be different for each returned missionary. Your challenges may be more difficult than others, but the way to rise above those challenges is the same. You must continue to have the Spirit of the Lord always guiding you. You received that promise when you were baptized and you receive it again each week as you partake of the sacrament. You can rely on that promise as you live worthily and keep the commandments of the Lord.

Your parents can also be a source of strength and nourishment to you. Seek priesthood blessings from your father if he is able to give them, or from another priesthood leader if not. Also, seek your parents' counsel and advice about problems you are facing. Elder M. Russell Ballard counseled, "I want to talk to all of you returned missionaries. . . . Trust your father. You can be closer to him now than ever before regardless of what your relationship was like before your mission."[24] Talk to your parents regularly, even if you are away from home. Keep that relationship alive in your life and you will find great strength from it, especially during times of challenge.

The most powerful spiritual experiences you will have in your life did not happen on your mission. Many are yet to come as you continue to grow, preparing for the future and striving to live the doctrine of Christ. The best way to rise above challenges in your life is to seek the guidance of the Lord and to seek the guidance and support of priesthood leaders, parents, family, and righteous friends.

Suggestions for Parents

My daughter went to Santiago, Chile, and loved it. She had an incredible experience. She didn't want to talk about coming home. She didn't want to make any plans about coming home. All of her plans were about the missionary work she was doing. Well, the day came when she came home. I noticed after a little bit that she was a little down. She finally said, "When can I go back? I'd love to go back and be with those people and feel needed and wanted and a part of their lives like I've been for the past year and a half." She had to fill that void back in her regular life. She needed to attend her ward and receive different callings and responsibilities. . . . Finally, she was called as a teacher and began to have some friends in her ward again.

> ➤ MOTHER OF A RETURNED MISSIONARY

INTERVIEW YOUR RETURNED MISSIONARY

When your returned missionary comes home, they will want to talk about their mission. Let them talk; enjoy listening to their stories. Soon after the celebrations die down, you may want to take them into a quiet room to ask them certain questions in private and to carefully listen to their answers. In order to prepare for this interview, you will need to ask the Lord for His Spirit to know what to say and how to listen. *Preach My Gospel* teaches about the importance of seeking the Spirit when asking questions: "Learn to ask questions as prompted by the Spirit. The right type of question at the right time can greatly help [your returned missionary]. . . . Asking appropriate questions at the right time requires that you are in tune with the Spirit."[25]

Listening with the Spirit is just as important. *Preach My Gospel* teaches, "When you listen carefully to others, you understand them better. When they know that their thoughts and feelings are important to you, they are more likely to be receptive to your teachings, share personal experiences, and make commitments."[26] In Elder M. Russell Ballard's talk, "Fathers and Sons: A Remarkable Relationship," he makes a strong point about fathers listening to their returned missionary sons:

> Fathers, listen to your sons—really listen to them. Ask the right kind of questions, and listen to what your sons have to say each time you have a few minutes together. You need to know—not to guess but to know—what is going on in your son's life. Don't assume that you know how he feels just because you were young once. Your sons live in a very different world from the one in which you grew up. As they share with you what's going on, you will have to listen very carefully and without being judgmental in order to understand what they are thinking and experiencing.[27]

Elder Ballard's advice is as important for daughters as it is for sons. Whether you have a returned missionary son or daughter, you may want to consider fasting before this interview to be directed by the Spirit as you ask questions and listen. Here are a few questions you may consider asking in this important interview:

- **How do you feel you have changed on your mission?** This question gives your returned missionary an opportunity to express all that has changed inside of him or her.

- **What new talents or strengths do you feel you've acquired while on your mission?** Each mission is different and each mission experience is different. You may be surprised as your missionary details newly acquired abilities.

- **Are there ways that you would like us to treat you differently now that you are back from your mission?** Now that you understand how they have changed, allow them to express what they would like you to do to help them keep these changes in their life. Listen carefully to their answer. Your returned missionary may feel reticent to be honest. Make them feel comfortable and assure them that you are ready to change, too.

- **What can we do as parents to help make this transition easier?** Ask this question with sincerity and real intent. Your missionary needs to feel that you are committed to helping them with this transition. By listening carefully to their answer, you will know what you can do to help them overcome challenges related to their return.

- **How can we change our family environment to support the changes you've experienced on your mission?** If your returned missionary is feeling comfortable in this interview, you may be surprised by the answers you receive to this question. They most certainly will not want to offend you, so please do not become offended if they point out improvements that could be made in your family environment. If you do, this will cause them to close up and feel like they can't talk to you anymore. You need to be sincerely interested in any suggestions they give you. Realize that they have been in many hundreds of homes and have seen good and bad examples of environments that can help or hinder families. Be receptive to their thoughts and feelings; your family will be better for it.

- **Is there anything you were working on with your mission president before you came home that we could help you with?** This is another question that requires great sensitivity with your returned missionary. Do not be shocked or surprised if there are still issues they are working on; some might be ones they had before the mission. You must continue to be supportive and helpful in the repentance process as your returned missionary continues towards perfection. You will want to regularly follow up with your returned missionary to aid their change. You may want to ask them how often their mission president followed up with them and how often they would like you to do so. They do not have a companion now. So, you may take on that role of reminding them daily what they need to do in order to overcome these challenges in their life.

Elder Ballard also offered the following counsel to fathers, which may be applied to daughters as well as sons: "Dare to have the 'big talks' with your sons [and daughters]. You know what I mean: talks about drugs and drinking, about the dangers of today's media—the Internet, cyber technologies, and pornography—and about priesthood worthiness, respect for [members of the opposite sex], and moral cleanliness. . . . As you talk about these very important matters, you will find that the trust between you will flourish."[28] The type of questions suggested above, accompanied by spirit-directed listening, can actually prevent challenges from arising in your returned missionary's life. They will feel loved when challenges do arise and will know that they can come to you to talk about their feelings, concerns, and worries without any judgment, anger, resentment, or disappointment.

GIVE YOUR RETURNED MISSIONARY
A PRIESTHOOD BLESSING

After your interview, give your missionary a priesthood blessing to help rise above the challenges and concerns that will surely be encountered. If there is not a worthy priesthood holder in your home, ask your bishop or home teacher to do it for you. Receiving a priesthood blessing is an essential step in their coming home experience, but it does not need to be a one-time event. Instead, pray with them regularly and be a positive example to them of employing the priesthood to bless their lives. Follow up regularly if there are issues or problems that arise in their lives. Ask them if they need another blessing and be willing to support their spiritual needs.

DEVELOP CHRISTLIKE ATTRIBUTES
WITHIN OURSELVES AS PARENTS

Our wonderful returned missionaries are still developing Christlike attributes in their lives. As their parents, we should continue to change and improve, too. The "Attribute Activity" on page 126 of *Preach My Gospel* asks you to read fifty-seven statements and decide how true each statement is about you. As you honestly analyze each of these characteristics in your life, you can easily determine those areas you need to improve.

Don't feel discouraged after doing this activity—everyone has areas that need improving. Instead, pick one of the areas where you scored lowest and focus on that one attribute. The attributes highlighted in this chapter include faith, hope, charity and love, virtue, knowledge, patience, humility, diligence, and obedience. Within the chapter's pages, each of these attributes is reviewed in greater detail, with scriptures to study and thought-provoking questions to ask yourself.

This activity is one your missionary probably did multiple times on the mission. You may enjoy sharing your journey of self-improvement and self-discovery with them. Having gone through the same process themselves, they will be able to relate to what you are doing, and you will come to understand better what they have gone through, while you both work together to improve.

FOLLOW ALMA THE YOUNGER'S EXAMPLE AND TEACHINGS

Alma the younger's story of conversion was described earlier in this book. He understood the power of repentance and the Atonement because he had personally experienced it. He taught the members of the Church of Jesus Christ these same principles with great power, especially when he observed that they were stagnating and not progressing forward. His mode of instruction was to ask soul-searching questions upon which the members could inwardly reflect (see Alma 5). This inner reflection coupled with prayer and fasting caused many members of the Church in Alma's day to change their ways, repent, and rededicate themselves to the gospel of Jesus Christ.

As members of Christ's Church today, you can use these same questions to understand, through the inspiration of the Spirit, the changes you must make to effectively help and strengthen your returned missionary. As stated at the beginning of this section for parents, your missionary's return is the perfect opportunity to assess and improve your family's spiritual standing as well as your own. Ask yourself:

- "Have ye spiritually been born of God?

- "Have ye received his image in your countenances?

- "Have ye experienced this mighty change in your hearts?

- "Do ye exercise faith in the redemption of him who created you?

- "Do you look forward with an eye of faith, and view this mortal body raised in immortality . . . to stand before God to be judged according to the deeds which have been done in the mortal body?

- "If ye have experienced a change of heart, and if ye have felt to sing the song of redeeming love, I would ask, can ye feel so now?

- "Have ye walked, keeping yourselves blameless before God?"[29]

Christ's invitation to "follow me"[30] is not only to missionaries who are now serving or who have returned. The invitation is to all of us—especially to us as parents!

NOTES

1. Personal letter.
2. Henry B. Eyring, "Mountains to Climb," *Ensign, May* 2012.
3. Ibid.
4. *Preach My Gospel* (Salt Lake City, Utah: The Church of Jesus Christ of Latter-day Saints, 2004), 73.
5. John 14:26.
6. 2 Nephi 32:5.
7. Doctrine and Covenants 11:27.
8. Doctrine and Covenants 11:13–14.
9. Doctrine and Covenants 11:19.
10. Doctrine and Covenants 9:7–8.
11. Doctrine and Covenants 6:15, 23.
12. Richard G. Scott, "To Acquire Spiritual Knowledge," *Ensign,* November 2009.
13. Kevin W. Pearson, "Stay by the Tree," *Ensign,* May 2015.
14. Scott, "To Acquire Spiritual Knowledge."
15. Pearson, "Stay by the Tree."
16. *Preach My Gospel,* 188–89.
17. Ibid., 189.
18. Ibid., 115.
19. Gordon B. Hinckley, "Find the Lambs, Feed the Sheep," *Ensign*, May 1999.
20. Marianne Holman Prescott, "Returned Missionaries Need a Friend, a Responsibility, and Spiritual Nourishment," *Church News,* February 18, 2014.

21. Ibid.

22. Ibid.

23. Doctrine and Covenants 43:34.

24. M. Russell Ballard, "Fathers and Sons: A Remarkable Relationship," *Ensign*, November 2009.

25. *Preach My Gospel*, 184.

26. Ibid., 185.

27. Ballard, "Fathers and Sons."

28. Ibid.

29. Alma 5:14–15, 26–27.

30. Matthew 4:19.

I had to come home from my mission after serving for fourteen months. Before there was an official diagnosis for my illness (they thought I might have diabetes) my mission president called me into his office and let me know I would almost certainly have to go home. I was heart-broken. All I had really looked forward to for the previous three years was being able to serve as a full-time missionary. That night was one of the most heart wrenching and yet spiritual nights of my life. As I prayed, I experienced a profound sense of peace. I didn't know exactly how everything was going to turn out, but I knew everything would be okay. The next day I found out I had leukemia and that I would definitely be going home. However, from the assurance I received the previous night, I knew everything would somehow work out. In fact, as difficult as all of the treatments would end up being, I always felt a reassuring peace that all would be well. As a result, when I reflect back on the experience, I think the most difficult aspect of the experience was finding out I had to leave the mission, not battling leukemia.

> RETURNED MISSIONARY ELDER

Coming Home Early

When you left on your mission, the possibility of coming home early was not even in your mind. Instead, you were anticipating an exciting spiritual adventure. You may have read the Lord's descriptions of missionary service and had high expectations for what was ahead:

- "And blessed are you because you have believed; And more blessed are you because you are called of me to preach my gospel."[1]

- "Open your mouths and they shall be filled, and you shall become even as Nephi of old, who journeyed from Jerusalem in the wilderness."[2]

- "Lo, he that thrusteth in his sickle with his might, the same layeth up in store that he perisheth not, but bringeth salvation to his soul."[3]

- "For I will go before your face. I will be on your right hand and on your left, and my Spirit shall be in your hearts, and mine angels round about you, to bear you up."[4]

All of these promises are as true for you as they are for every missionary who serves, whether it is for the entire term of eighteen months to two years or for only part of that time. These promises are for all who embark on the service of their God.

COMING HOME EARLY FOR EMOTIONAL PROBLEMS

You may have come home for reasons beyond your control. You may have struggled with emotional or mental health issues previously and thought you could manage them during your mission because you had been stable previously for many months or even years. Or, as with many other missionaries, you may not have had any earlier problems in these areas, but the pressure and stress of missionary service caused them to manifest on the mission. Neither you nor the missionary department could have foreseen what would happen under the stress, strain, and rigors of missionary service.

Thomas was a missionary in Virginia. He had a history of emotional issues, which he indicated on his mission papers. He was interviewed and assessed before he was sent out in the mission field. The anxiety that had troubled him in his teens was amplified in the mission environment. Being cut off from communication with his family was very difficult for him since his family had been the mainstay that had helped him successfully manage anxiety in the past. He also struggled serving in the Bible Belt where his belief system was constantly challenged. He said, "After ten months of being in Virginia in three different areas, I was finally so debilitated that just getting up and studying was terrifying. I was just broken."[5]

Chad also had struggled with anxiety and depression in his teens. He was called to the New York Rochester Mission and entered the MTC feeling mentally strong and fit. He said, "I felt really good. The first few days I didn't feel at all anxious or depressed. I didn't feel any type of homesickness. I was made a district leader the first day in and had a really good experience with my district and my companion. And then at the end of the first week it just hit me. I was feeling super anxious, getting all those symptoms back again. I didn't know what was going on."[6]

He did return home the day before his district left for New York. He talked about his return home, "I came home and I was like, 'This is super weird.' I hadn't had the whole two-year experience by any means. I felt out of place. It was difficult seeing my family because I don't think they understood what I was going through, what depression and anxiety were or how I was dealing with it."[7]

Karen's story is a bit different since she did not have any known mental health issues before entering the MTC. Her mother tells her story:

Karen was diagnosed with Acute Anxiety Distress Disorder toward the end of her training in the Provo MTC. In hindsight, she probably showed some tendencies while she was still in high school. . . . Well-structured and consistent expectations do not cause Karen's severe anxiety, but unforeseen obstacles, unreasonable demands, and abrupt changes in circumstances are her triggers. She experienced many of these in a short amount of time while in the MTC. Visa delays, new assignments, frequently changing departure dates, and unknown travel plans created mounting anxiety. . . . This is an exceptional young woman with a wonderful testimony of the gospel and the desire to do all that is right. But, when stressful situations surfaced, she responded with "fight or flight," which is characteristic of this disorder. I consider it a tender mercy that she did go through this trial at this time in her life because now, with medication and after wise counseling, she lives a happy and productive life with a wonderful family of her own.[8]

For each of these returned missionaries, their service will continue to bless their lives forever. The same is true for you! You need to celebrate your service whether it lasted thirty-six hours, two months, or twenty months. The Lord honors those who serve Him, and lovingly judges them not only according to their works, but "according to the desire of their hearts."[9] As you return home, the Savior still promises you: "My Spirit shall be in your hearts, and mine angels round about you, to bear you up."[10]

COMING HOME EARLY FOR PHYSICAL PROBLEMS

During his last two years of high school, Scott worked making shipping crates at a machine shop. While nailing a lid on a crate, the nail gun double fired—the first nail went into the crate and the second into Scott's left femur, just above the knee. The nail pinned his leg at a ninety degree angle and he couldn't straighten his leg. He lay alone on the ground unable to move until he heard a car door of someone who worked in an adjacent building. He asked the man to call his dad and to call 911.

After receiving the proper medical care, Scott thought his leg was completely healed. He completed his mission papers and received a call to the Guatemala City South Mission. He had been in Guatemala for about two months when, one day, as he and his companion were visiting investigators, his left knee gave out and couldn't hold his weight. Being about an hour's walk from home, his companion supported him all the way back. Scott also lost his appetite. He lost all the weight he had put on in the MTC and he continued losing weight fast. The only thing he could eat was fresh bananas.

In a blur of events over a couple days, Scott's mission plans and life-long dreams seemed to be pulled away from him against his will. He was so sick he needed to be sent home immediately. He was sad he didn't get to say goodbye to the members or investigators in his first and only area where he had served a total of two months.

After returning home, Scott returned to see the same doctor who had treated his initial leg injury. That doctor was unsure of what to do and recommended exploratory surgery. Scott's bishop strongly suggested a second opinion and arranged for him to see one of the nation's premier orthopedic surgeons. This doctor determined that the nail gun injury, which penetrated through his femur into his marrow, had not been properly cleaned. The initial doctor had only prescribed a routine dose of oral antibiotics when a larger, intravenous dose should have been administered for a longer period of time. Scott had developed a bone infection, which had caused damage to his knee and had taken away his appetite.

Scott felt like a failure. He felt he had let down his mission, his family, and even God. He was embarrassed to leave his home out of fear that he would see high school friends who knew he had left for a mission just months ago. He was ashamed to go to Church where his mission plaque still hung on the wall.

As soon as possible, Scott underwent surgery. Once discharged, they inserted a pick line to administer stronger antibiotics into his blood. He was confined to bed while a machine moved his leg in a circular motion all day long. He had months of rehabilitation to recover from this infection and corrective surgery. He remained set apart as a missionary until one day the physical therapist wanted him to do therapy in a swimming pool. Since missionaries aren't allowed to swim, Scott was released. That was another blow to Scott's self-esteem and he began to wonder if he would be able to serve a full-time mission again.

Scott was finally cleared to return on his mission after months of rehabilitation. Because of his medical condition, he was reassigned to a state-side mission. He assumed he would go to Texas or Southern California where he would continue to teach in Spanish. He received a phone call with his new assignment and was stunned to learn he was being sent to Birmingham, Alabama. Scott did not realize that the mission president in Alabama had recently requested medically reassigned missionaries who spoke Spanish to be assigned to his mission. The president realized that there were many Hispanic people in Alabama who needed to hear the gospel.

Scott loved his mission in Alabama as much as he loved his mission in Guatemala and he truly loved the people in both. He had experiences in both missions that changed his life. He felt he was a better missionary in Alabama because of what he had been through. Being able to teach both English- and Spanish-speaking investigators, he found endless opportunities to teach the gospel. The physical pain and spiritual trial of coming home were a small price to pay for the blessings he saw on his continued mission and in his life afterward.

You may have had health issues develop while on your mission. Whether these issues were because of an injury, a disease, or an accident, if your president determined that they were going to take time to heal, sending you home was actually a blessing to you and to the progress of the work in your mission. You may not have thought so when it happened, but in retrospect, and in striving to see the situation as the Lord sees it, you will come to understand more fully, and the Spirit will speak peace to your soul. Through your healing you may gain a deeper understanding of the Atonement than you ever had before. Remember that physical pains and suffering may be borne and overcome through the power of the Atonement, just as spiritual pains and suffering are.[11] There is also the matter of your companions and the work that they could accomplish, equally yoked with another missionary who is healthy and able to work hard instead of being stuck in their apartment for days, weeks, or even months.

Chase was a healthy young man who enjoyed sports and the outdoors. He was excited about going on a mission and looked forward to serving in Brazil. While serving in a coastal city, Chase became very sick after drinking the water there. He had contracted encephalitis. The Brazilian doctors could do little to help him because it was a viral infection. If he were under tension or stress, the problem would return and worsen. Chase returned home and continued treatment under a doctor's care. He did get better, but he was not well enough to complete his mission. Chase decided to continue with his life and went back to school. Even though he went home early, he continued his purpose by staying active in the Church, marrying a beautiful young woman in the temple, and starting an eternal family.

Physical difficulties from the mission often take time to heal. Healing needs to be your number one focus while you are home, not worrying about if or when you will return. That will all work out according to the Lord's will and timetable, and He will guide you and your leaders to make the right decision at the right time. The Lord knows your heart and your desire to be a missionary. As with mental and emotional issues, when physical problems prohibit the full completion of a mission, your intentions and desires become the basis for your standing before the Lord. He has said, "For I, the Lord, will judge all men according to their works, according to the desire of their hearts."[12] The Lord understands your feelings and accepts the offering of those who desire to serve as well as those who actually serve.

As an early returned missionary with physical problems, realize that patience is an essential virtue during these trials. You may heal and return to service, or you may never get completely better. In any event, the Savior will still strengthen your faith during this time and eventually confirm the right path for you. You must remember that He has declared, "ye receive no witness until after the trial of your faith,"[13] but that witness will surely come! Your faith will increase as you rely upon your Savior to help you during these trials.

COMING HOME EARLY FOR WORTHINESS ISSUES

In a Brigham Young University–Idaho Devotional, President Kim Clark told the story of a young man he called Michael. Michael was so excited to be going on a mission and felt a wonderful spirit on his first day at the MTC. That spirit touched his soul so deeply that some things began to surface that had been hidden and buried for a long time. Before long, the guilt weighed him down until he knew he had to speak to the president of the MTC. The decision was made that Michael should go home. Over nine months, Michael repented. It was a difficult process, but he felt a "mighty change" in his heart.[14] He got a job, worked with his bishop, read his scriptures regularly, prayed often, and served in his ward. President Clark observed: "Michael returned to the temple and to the mission field. His mission was not easy, but he served faithfully and well. He became a mighty elder in Israel."[15]

While it is certainly far better to have fully repented from transgressions before going on a mission, there is rejoicing in heaven when a beloved son or daughter of Heavenly Father repents and begins to apply the Atonement in his or her life. If you returned from your mission for such a reason, the most important thing you can do is to seek humbly and prayerfully to feel the love that your Heavenly Father has for you, to let that love permeate your being, and to let it impel you to repent fully and to be cleansed by the sanctifying power of the Holy Ghost.

Although there may be family, friends, or ward members who react in a less than charitable way to your return, you must remember that as you seek the Lord's forgiveness, you must also forgive others. He has declared that: "inasmuch as you have forgiven one another your trespasses, even so I, the Lord, forgive you."[16] Be positive as you interact with others. Remember that as you let virtue garnish your thoughts unceasingly, your "confidence [will] wax strong in the presence of God."[17] With that confidence your countenance will begin to shine, others will see it, and it will influence them for good—and you will become the great missionary the Lord has called you to be!

Describing the missionary who truly repents, President Kimball has said that he then "goes into the mission field with a light heart, with full freedom and assurance. He has acted voluntarily to free himself. His confession and the resultant forgiveness bring security and rich rewards."[18] Finally, remember always to treasure in your heart these words, referring to how your Savior feels about you: "How great is his joy in the soul that repenteth!"[19]

THE WOUNDED WARRIOR

The armies of Helaman fought hard to protect the city of Cumeni. Their families had already played an important part in strengthening them while they were in battle. Earlier, an additional sixty warriors had joined them, providing them with new strength, needed food, supplies, and news from home.[20] After the battle was over, their families continued to play an important part, especially in helping these young men heal from the many wounds they had suffered.

During this intense battle, 200 of Helaman's 2,060 young warriors "had fainted because of the loss of blood" and "there was not one soul . . . among them who had not received many wounds."[21] It is likely that their fellow soldiers, their leaders, and possibly even some of their parents came to help bind up their wounds, preparing them to return to fight. Some of them were probably too hurt to return to the battlefield. They needed to return home to heal and have their wounds looked at by professional healers. Those who had to return home early were still acclaimed as valiant warriors. Their wounds did not diminish the perception others had of their bravery and courage.

Aaron Olsen, an early returned missionary, found a great deal of comfort from a similar war analogy. He has pointed out how the military views wounded comrades in arms and their ability to finish their military mission quite differently from his experience as a missionary who returned early. When a soldier is wounded, whether it is their first or their fiftieth mission, they are treated the same. Aaron has observed, "They are given medals. They are applauded for their service, no matter how long. Their brothers and sisters at arms risk their own lives to rescue and restore those soldiers to their homes. No one looks at them differently. No one says, 'Well, you didn't really help the war effort, did you?' or 'Toughen up, man. It's just a bullet.' These brave men and women are honored and respected for their service. So should it be with missionaries."[22]

As a missionary coming home before the end of full-time service, you will also need your wounds cared for and bound up with the help of professional healers, family, and friends. Each situation is different, just as it was with the wounded stripling warriors of the armies of Helaman, and will require great care and the help of the Spirit to make the right decisions before returning to missionary service, or perhaps back to work or school. Remember that your service was just as meaningful as that of other missionaries. While you may have come home wounded in some way, you are still to be honored for the service you have rendered.

FOCUS ON HEALING

No matter why you were sent home, you need to heal. This must be your first priority! You may need to heal physically, emotionally, spiritually, or sometimes, in all three ways. You have to work through this trial. You can't push it aside and simply ignore it. Otherwise, the problem may come back to hurt you over and over again. Don't doubt that you have enough faith to be healed, but remember that you may also need to have enough faith *not* to be healed, or at least not right away. In other words, you need to be able to go on even if you aren't healed, and then find out what the Lord needs you to do.

Remember that there are "triggers" that can set off your emotions. These emotional triggers can come in all shapes and sizes and you may not see them coming. This reaction is normal and will get better with time. One missionary who returned early talked about how difficult it was for him to read his scriptures. Every time he saw a scripture he had used with an investigator or a comment he wrote in the margins of his scriptures from a zone conference, he felt depressed. The scriptures became his emotional trigger. It did not help that all his friends and family kept pushing him to keep reading his scriptures. Every time he read them, he felt himself going down deeper and deeper into an emotional place from which he couldn't lift himself out. Finally, he received counseling and read some religious books, which helped him increase his spirituality without the emotional triggers. Time was his healer and he was able to return to reading his scriptures again.

A family psychologist who works with such missionaries related, "One of the things I hear all the time is that spiritual things remind them of their mission. Reading the scriptures and praying reminds them of when they did that on their mission, so they develop an aversion to the very things that could be spiritually helping or healing them."[23]

Healing can also be promoted by talking to a counselor or a support group with others who are going through a similar experience. Ask your bishop or stake president about options for finding counseling.

THE MISSION THE LORD HAS PLANNED FOR YOU

You never know what mission the Lord has planned for you. It might not be the one you were originally called to serve. The missionary in the story at the beginning of this chapter found out he had cancer and had to return home early to start chemo and radiation treatments. Leaving his mission was more difficult than battling the cancer. While he was in the hospital, he met with other people who were going through cancer treatments. Many of them had questions about what would happen if they died. He was able to teach the plan of salvation to them and baptized a young man and his family whom he had met at the cancer treatment center.

An American missionary in Brazil had an accident while on his mission which meant he needed to go home immediately for surgery. When he returned home, he found out the missionaries in his home ward had two families who spoke Portuguese that wanted to learn about the gospel.

None of the missionaries in his home mission could speak Portuguese. He was able to teach these families while recuperating from his operation.

One American sister missionary was unable to finish her mission for emotional and medical reasons. While she was on her mission, she met a young Brazilian returned missionary. She started writing this young man after she returned home and was released from full-time missionary service. They courted and were later married in the temple in São Paulo, Brazil. They have been happily married ever since and she loves living in Brazil.

Another sister missionary was coming home early and was stuck in Dallas due to thunderstorms. She watched two young Mormon elders Bible-bashing with an older gentleman. The situation was becoming hostile and this upset her. The elders finally got tired of this activity and left to find something to eat. The sister went over to this man and started a conversation. He was on the defensive from his earlier encounter with the elders. She simply asked what he believed in and a conversation started. She discovered that the man thought the LDS religion taught that, without works, there was no grace. She explained that all of God's children are saved through the Atonement, but that works are required because we are needed to help His children and spread His gospel. He said he now understood.

Then she introduced him to the Book of Mormon and explained briefly what this inspired book was about. The man was amazed to learn that Jesus visited the Nephites in the American continent. Previously, he could not understand how a loving Savior would only be concerned with one corner of the world. This sister witnessed that this was not so, and all the earlier anger and contention dissipated. He willingly accepted the book and boarded his flight. This experience was fundamental to helping this lovely sister feel like her missionary calling had been validated.

The Lord loves you. You may not be able to see that now, but He does. Write in a journal regularly about what you are feeling, how people are helping you, and what you are doing each day. As you write, try to notice the Lord's hand in the actions of the people around you who are helping you and keeping you moving forward. "Why" questions are not helpful and often don't get answered. Instead, start asking "What" questions while you are writing and see if you find the answers (for example, What can I learn from this? What should I do next in my life?).

Find good things to be involved in, such as institute, humanitarian projects, temple attendance, volunteer work at the MTC, exercise, church service, working at the bishops' storehouse, serving neighbors and friends, and writing letters to other missionaries and former investigators. Make sure you stay on a schedule. Plan out your days and fill them with good and uplifting activities. Use a planner like you did when you were a missionary and continue to have a primary plan and a backup plan for each hour of the day.

THE PARABLE OF THE LABORER

The Savior taught the parable of the laborer during his ministry in Jerusalem. The Lord of the vineyard agreed to pay the first laborers a penny for the day's work, and to those hired later, he promised "whatsoever is right."[24] At the end of the day, the laborers were called by the Lord to receive their wages, and astonishingly, he gave them each the same amount for "they likewise received every man a penny."[25] Those who had labored longer complained, supposing that they should have received a higher wage. They argued, "These last have wrought but one hour, and thou hast made them equal unto us, which have borne the burden and heat of the day."[26] The Lord answered them, "Friend, I do thee no wrong: didst not thou agree with me for a penny? Take that thine is, and go thy way: I will give unto this last, even as unto thee. Is it not lawful for me to do what I will with mine own?"[27]

Elder Jeffrey R. Holland used this parable to help us, as the Lord's laborers, to understand the importance of not comparing our service to that of others: "We are not in a race against each other to see who is the wealthiest or the most talented or the most beautiful or even the most blessed. The race we are *really* in is the race against sin, and surely envy is one of the most universal of those. . . . Coveting, pouting, or tearing others down does *not* elevate *your* standing, nor does demeaning someone else improve your self-image. So be kind, and grateful that God is kind. It is a happy way to live."[28]

Missionaries who come home early need to be kind to themselves and to others as they reflect on the privilege that was theirs to serve the Lord for as long as they were able. There is no reason for guilt or shame. The Lord will richly recompense you for whatever service you gave as well as for the additional service you desired to give. You must simply continue in His service, however, whenever, and wherever you are able!

SOCIAL CHALLENGES AND SPIRITUAL CHALLENGES

There are definitely social and spiritual challenges in the life of a missionary who comes home early. For example, you may feel embarrassed to go back to your home ward. You don't know how people in the ward will react to you and you worry about what they are thinking or saying behind your back.

One missionary who returned early commented that he became a recluse because he did not feel like seeing people. He was worried that they would start asking him questions about why he was home. In his mind, he felt apprehensive about members speculating on the reason for his return and stereotyping him. He commented, "I was apprehensive about going to church, too. No one wanted to approach or talk to me at first."

People often don't know what to say to you. They may be worried about offending you, so they will shy away or say nothing. This is a chance for you to use the skills you learned on your mission to "break the ice" and to interact personally and lovingly with others. This will take some courage on your part, but with practice, you can quickly relieve much of the stress and awkwardness that you and those you meet may feel.

Practice a few simple but direct and appropriate ways of greeting others. These should always begin with a warm and friendly opening such as "How are you? It's good to see you . . ." Before they can begin to ask questions, proceed quickly to say something like, "I know you're probably surprised to see me, but I've had to come home because of a medical issue that I'm dealing with. I don't yet know if or when I'll be able to return, but I just want to do whatever the Lord wants me to do." In making such a brief statement, you've conveyed three important points: (1) why you're back, (2) you don't know if or when you'll return, and (3) you are committed to doing the Lord's will. That last point will be especially effective in preemptively answering any other questions they may have been tempted to ask. You can always reiterate that point if they insist on asking additional questions. Since emotional or mental health issues may also be characterized as "medical issues," that one simple phrase can accurately and honestly cover any number of reasons why you have returned early.

The one remaining situation that may be difficult to explain is coming home early for a worthiness issue. In this case, it is especially important not to go into any details—it is simply not appropriate. The best and simplest way to deal with such a case is perhaps to change the "why" line suggested above to something like, "I've had to come home early to prepare myself better so that I can serve the Lord as effectively as possible."

The above suggestions are simply that—suggestions. Be sure to counsel with your parents, your bishop and/or your stake president about what you might say and how to say it. Don't hesitate to review it again later with them as you move forward and the situation progresses. Above all, pray to be guided by the Holy Ghost and to be filled with charity for those with whom you will interact.

HANDLING "WHAT HAPPENS NEXT" DECISIONS

As you stay close to the Lord, He will help you and guide you as you prayerfully consider, "What should I do next?" This can be a tricky question because for each missionary the answer will be different. Too often, you may feel bombarded with the question, "When are you going back on your mission?" Perhaps you will be able to go back to your same mission. Or you may return to full-time missionary service, but be reassigned to another mission. If you want to continue to serve, but for whatever reason cannot return to full-time missionary service, you may, with the help of your priesthood leaders, investigate other opportunities serving as a Church service missionary near your home. Depending on circumstances, you may not be able to return to missionary service at all, and it is important to know and feel that you have fulfilled your missionary obligation to the Lord.

You need to make the decision as to which path is right for you. Your decision is between you and the Lord, with counsel and guidance from your parents and priesthood leaders.

You can be creative in looking for other opportunities to serve if the healing process is taking longer than anticipated or if you are unable to return to your mission. Instead of the traditional knocking-on-doors mission, you can fulfill a Church service mission, a temple mission, or a ward mission. These options should be considered prayerfully as you counsel with your bishop.

THE POWER OF THE ATONEMENT

The Lord knows your heart and understands how you feel. He said, "all among them who know their hearts are honest, and are broken, and their spirits contrite, and are willing to observe their covenants by sacrifice—yea, every sacrifice which I, the Lord, shall command—they are accepted of me."[29] You are acceptable to Him and your missionary service is acceptable to Him, too!

No matter your circumstance or why you came home early, you must keep the Lord in your life. Remember that He has not abandoned you, but will help you become an even better, stronger person than before. Elder Holland bore a strong testimony of the Lord's divine love for you:

"I testify that you have *not* traveled beyond the reach of divine love. It is not possible for you to sink lower than the infinite light of Christ's Atonement shines. . . . There is no problem which you cannot overcome. There is no dream that in the unfolding of time and eternity cannot yet be realized. Even if you feel you are the lost and last laborer of the eleventh hour, the Lord of the vineyard still stands beckoning."[30]

THIS BOOK IS FOR YOU, TOO!

You may feel different from other returned missionaries, but you shouldn't. You served the Lord as a missionary. You are a returned missionary. The fact that you came home early should not follow you around, especially after you have healed from the reasons for which you returned. The principles in this book are for you, too, and will help you with your transition home, whether or not you will return to full-time missionary service. Remember that the Lord has promised, "I will be with you."[31]

Suggestions for Parents

For medical reasons, our daughter was unable to complete her assigned mission. She came back with some stress and with some real medical concerns that we were not prepared to handle right off the bat. Fortunately, through counseling and a lot of love and acceptance, we were able to walk her through this and now she leads a normal life.

When she first returned home, she was completely discouraged. Emotionally, she was depressed and she had a lot of self-doubt. It was a major challenge for us to work with her. In order to help her through this time, we had to give her a lot of reassurance, going with her to counseling and following the guidance the counselor gave her and us in order to completely restore her self-image.

The most important thing she needed was to feel the reassurance of the love of the Savior and His acceptance of her as a missionary and as a daughter of God—that it was okay, she had done her best, and He was pleased with her efforts.

> ➤ FATHER OF A RETURNED MISSIONARY

If you are the parent of a missionary who came home early, you may find that you don't know how to feel about the situation. You may not be sure if you should feel happy, sad, disappointed, or ashamed. It is common to feel all of these emotions in such circumstances, although if you've read the previous section to missionaries, you'll know that you need not have negative feelings—there is really so much to be positive about! What is most important, though, is how your missionary is feeling. Whether they came home early because of physical health issues, mental health issues, or transgressions, they need to feel your unconditional love. They must know that they are accepted back into your home with open arms.

THE TRAUMA OF COMING HOME EARLY

The unexpected challenge of coming home early from a mission can be psychologically and emotionally traumatic both for missionaries and for their families. All have been looking forward to the full culmination of missionary service with its homecoming speeches, balloons and banners, the multitude of expressions for a job well done, and the personal pronouncement by the missionaries themselves that "these were the best years of my life."

Dr. Kris Doty is an assistant professor of social work at Utah Valley University and the mother of two returned missionaries who came home early. She decided to spearhead a study of 348 young men and women using an anonymous survey. Even though her study does not represent all of the returned missionaries throughout the Church, her study does reveal some interesting statistics:

> Despite social stigma, most early-returned missionaries don't come home because of unresolved transgression. More than a third—36 percent—came home because of mental health concerns, 34 percent for physical health concerns, 12 percent for unresolved transgression, and 11 percent for disobedience to mission rules. Of the total respondents, 39 percent reported that coming home was their personal choice. The length of time served also varied widely. Of the early-returned missionaries who took the survey, 40 percent served for longer than a year before they came home. Fifty percent said they "loved their missions."

Nearly two-thirds—62 percent—reported they had strong spiritual experiences on their mission. Despite success during their missions, however, 73 percent of early-returned missionaries in the survey experienced feelings of failure. A third (34 percent) had a period of inactivity in the Church when they came home, and one third of those missionaries stayed inactive and never returned to church activity.[32]

These are alarming numbers for the returned missionary group that Dr. Doty studied. Almost three-fourths of the returned missionaries she studied felt they were a failure and over a third had a period of inactivity from the Church after coming home, while one ninth stayed inactive. These facts are disturbing and disappointing for even this relatively small group of returned missionaries. Missionaries, families, ward members, and priesthood leaders all need to take responsibility for these elders and sisters who have served the Lord faithfully so they neither become lost nor feel forgotten. This is not a problem that will go away. The number of missionaries who come home early will continue to grow as the total number of missionaries continues to increase. As members of the Church, we need to find ways to support and help these young people and their families.

THE PHONE CALL

In our mission, an elder was at a ward party and fell in such a way that his knee joint locked into place. The doctor in the emergency room at a Brazilian hospital said he needed surgery, but the Church felt this elder would need a more experienced surgeon for this delicate procedure. The elder needed to go home immediately to the United States for the surgery. The phone call was a huge surprise to this family as they had just received his weekly email the day before telling them how wonderfully he was doing and how great his mission was.

When you receive the initial phone call from the mission president that your missionary is coming home early, you may be in shock. Sometimes, you may have been aware that your missionary and the mission president have been working together on an issue, but sometimes, the phone call can come as a complete surprise. Either way, the phone call will be difficult.

You will often have the opportunity to talk to your missionary at this point. First and foremost, remind them of how much you love them and of how proud you are of them and their service. Even if they have returned because of sin, they have made the first step in the repentance process. No matter the reason for coming home, you should contact your priesthood leaders immediately to make sure they have the information about your missionary's return.

After these phone calls, kneel down and pray before contacting family and friends to be directed by the Spirit as to what you should say. You may want to counsel with your bishop or stake president first, too, and review some possible ways of referring to your missionary's return. Some of the suggestions for how to speak with others that were mentioned in the section to missionaries earlier in this chapter may also be helpful to you. Seek for peace and healing for yourself as well as for your missionary. You may have many questions come into your mind like:

- Why did the Lord let this happen to my son or daughter? Why didn't the Lord protect my missionary?

- Could I have prevented this from happening? Was it my fault?

- As a parent, should I have seen some signs or had a spiritual feeling that this might happen?

- Did the Church make a mistake in sending my missionary to that mission?

- Does the Lord really love my missionary and me?

Realize that all those questions are the same ones your missionary has asked and will ask him or herself many times during the transition home. Go to the Lord, your priesthood leaders, and if needed, a professional counselor, if you feel the need for additional help and insights in answering these important spiritual questions. However, the one thing you can be absolutely sure of is that the Lord does love both your missionary and you, He wants what is best for both of you, and He will be with you, comforting and guiding you if you will let Him. As with most trials in this life, the reasons will often not be apparent until later, and sometimes not until we leave this life and are together again in the next.

YOUR IMPORTANT JOB

The most important job you have is to make your missionary feel loved and accepted. You can do this by treating them like you would any other returned missionary. Thank them for their service to the Lord, and ask them to share their missionary experiences with you. Psychologist Dr. Geret Giles has observed, "Early-returned missionaries often don't get a chance to share positive experiences they had on their mission. They have stories of conversion and personal experiences with the Spirit, but a lot of them don't get to share. Asking about their mission is really helpful for missionaries."[33]

Be careful of your words and the subliminal message your words may give to your missionary. One returned missionary said, "What early release missionaries do not need to hear is 'sorry.' We want to know that our sacrifice mattered. . . . For me, an arm around my shoulder, a 'Welcome home, Elder,' and a warm smile are all I ever wanted coming home."[34] Craig Moffat, a former mission president, commented, "The problems come when parents are defensive and angry. These feelings are quickly absorbed by the missionary. They think they're unworthy anyway. Tell them it's okay. Get them talking."[35]

You can help your missionary a great deal by being the one to tell other people that they are coming home and that you are thrilled to see them. Give as much detail about the reason for returning home as is appropriate and as your missionary and you feel comfortable giving. Again, you may find the suggestions for what to say cited earlier in this chapter to be helpful. Seek the Lord's guidance as you express your feelings to others about what has happened. Be careful not to say something initially that you may regret later. You can pass this information through an email or blog, but it is important to handle it in a manner that works best for your missionary and for you. By handling this information properly, you will save your missionary from having to repeat it over and over to friends and family, which they may find very painful.

Dr. Doty's research shows that missionaries coming home early "who don't feel welcome at Church are more likely to experience a period of inactivity" and struggle with their testimony. "Conversely, if ward members receive missionaries with warmth and friendliness, the adjustment is easier and missionaries are more likely to remain active in the Church." She also points out that even though most of the returned missionaries she studied are still strong and faithful in the Church, many of them still feel lingering shame for having come home early. Dr. Doty states, "We need to stop shaming people when they come home early from their missions. Shame has no place in this Church."[36]

CELEBRATE MISSIONARY SERVICE

Instead of focusing on the fact that your missionary returned early, you, your family, and your ward members need to celebrate the service they gave to the Lord. "Only in the Church do we get excited when we send somebody out for full-time service, then mourn if they serve for only eight months," said Dr. Doty. "What about the eight months [they] gave? That's eight months of [their] entire life! We gloss over it like it's not important."[37] Family members can still make the banners, blow up the balloons, and throw a party for their returning missionary (if they're up to it). Celebrate them when they return home!

The Lord accepts missionaries as His servants and agents whether their service lasted two years, two months, or two days. The Lord said, "Wherefore, as ye are agents, ye are on the Lord's errand; and whatever ye do according to the will of the Lord is the Lord's business."[38] These returned missionaries have served the Lord, doing His errand. Celebrate their service!

FOCUS ON THEIR HEALING AND ON YOUR HEALING

The early return of a missionary may cause those involved to feel depressed, overwhelmed, and alone. Usually, the missionary has experienced some kind of physical, emotional, or spiritual damage, which can be traumatic in and of itself. But the objective fact that such injury has occurred is not the only source of trauma. Instead, parents and the missionary may experience subjective emotional feelings that can have a much more negative effect. The more frightened and helpless one feels during the experience, the more likely one is to be traumatized by it.[39]

Just as your missionary's focus should be on healing, you should focus on helping them heal and receive the needed medical, emotional, or spiritual support. Help them make and keep appointments with doctors, mental health counselors, or priesthood leaders. Spend time talking with them and finding out how they are feeling about what is happening to them. Encourage, but don't pressure or be bossy!

It is very likely that you may need to heal, too. You had worked hard to prepare your missionary to go on a full-time mission. Now, that dream has changed. You may feel frustrated, concerned, betrayed, and even depressed over the different ending to your missionary's story. You may find spiritually positive discussions with others very therapeutic. If you find yourself needing additional help, your bishop can refer you to an LDS counselor who can help you find peace in the midst of this trial.

BE PATIENT

Patience is essential during this traumatic and emotional transition—patience both with yourself and with your missionary. Your missionary needs to talk through this difficult experience with someone, and that person may be someone other than you (such as a church leader or therapist). Encourage your missionary to find meaningful activities to do (as previously mentioned), including attending institute, doing humanitarian projects, attending or serving as an ordinance worker at the temple, exercising, volunteering at the MTC, helping at the bishops' storehouse, and teaching with missionaries in your hometown. These ideas will vary depending on your missionary's situation.

Your missionary may be very happy and well-adjusted one day and then in the depths of despair the next. Remember that there are "triggers" that will cause them to feel depressed and frustrated once more. These emotional triggers could be as simple as reading a scripture they were teaching one of their investigators just before they left or meeting a neighbor who makes a rude or unfeeling comment. These mood changes will require your patience so that you do not allow yourself to be affected by them. Instead, try to maintain a steady, patient, and concerned attitude.

Encourage them to write down their thoughts and experiences during this transition in a personal journal. Later, it will be very powerful for them to reflect back on how the Lord was with them and carried them through this difficult time. Help them to see the Lord's hand in their lives every day.

LET THEM HANDLE THEIR
"WHAT HAPPENS NEXT" DECISIONS

Realize that your missionary may not go back to full-time missionary service. The decision of "what happens next" can be tricky. Encourage them to seek the Lord's guidance and to counsel with their priesthood leaders on how to proceed in their situation. Each situation is different and the answer may be different, too. Do not assume you know what their decision will be. You can help them talk through their thoughts and feelings, but allow them to make the decision as to whether or when to return to their full-time mission.

Suggestions for Families

DON'T BE NOSEY OR CROSS-EXAMINE

If you are a brother or sister, you may want to know all the juicy details about why your missionary sibling is home early. Allow them to talk about it as much or as little as they want without pressure from you. If they want to talk about it, listen. If not, talk to them about something else that you would normally talk about, but make sure it is something positive and uplifting. Being natural and authentic in your conversations will eliminate any awkwardness. And never talk about them behind their back! Your family can help your missionary by fielding questions tactfully and without giving too much information.

SHOW LOVE

Make sure your missionary brother or sister feels love and support from you. They want to know that you still love them and that you are proud of the missionary service they gave to the Lord. Express those feelings sincerely. If you cannot express them sincerely, then pray for the Lord's help to do so. The Spirit will guide you to know what to say and how to act if you ask for His guidance.

In cases of a return because of transgression, the Savior gave us the perfect pattern of how to react in the story of the woman taken in adultery when he taught, "He that is without sin among you, let him first cast a stone at her."[40] Similarly, as a family you should never make judgments or condemn your missionary since none of us is perfect and we will stand "convicted by [our] own conscience."[41] Instead, the Savior has said that "great is his joy in the soul that repenteth."[42] So should you express your joy and support for your courageous returned missionary sibling who is willing to deeply and truly repent of past mistakes.

NOTES

1. Doctrine and Covenants 34:4–5.
2. Doctrine and Covenants 33:8.
3. Doctrine and Covenants 4:4.
4. Doctrine and Covenants 84:88.
5. "Early-Returned Missionaries Thrive With Acceptance, Love," Utah Valley 360, April 22, 2014, http://utahvalley360.com/2014/04/22/early-returned -missionaries.

6. Ibid.

7. Ibid.

8. Personal letter, January 25, 2014. While the missionary's name has been changed, I have quoted from the letter her mother sent to me. Karen and her mother wanted her story to be told.

9. Doctrine and Covenants 137:9.

10. Doctrine and Covenants 84:88.

11. Alma 7:11–12.

12. Doctrine and Covenants 137:9.

13. Ether 12:6.

14. Alma 5:14.

15. Kim B. Clark, "Follow the Son with Full Purpose of Heart," *BYU–Idaho Devotional*, April 17, 2007, http://www2.byui.edu/Presentations/Transcripts/Devotionals/2007_04_17_Clark.htm.

16. Doctrine and Covenants 82:1.

17. Doctrine and Covenants 121:45.

18. Spencer W. Kimball, *The Miracle of Forgiveness* (Salt Lake City, Utah: Bookcraft, 1969), 335.

19. Doctrine and Covenants 18:13.

20. See Alma 57:6.

21. Alma 57:25.

22. Aaron Olsen, "When a Missionary Returns Early," *LDS Living*, August, 5 2014, http://www.ldsliving.com/story/63954-when-a-missionary-returns-early/print.

23. "Early-Returned Missionaries Thrive with Acceptance, Love."

24. Matthew 20:4, 7.

25. Matthew 20:10.

26. Matthew 20:12.

27. Matthew 20:13–15.

28. Jeffrey R. Holland, "The Laborers in the Vineyard," *Ensign*, May 2012.

29. Doctrine and Covenants 97:8.

30. Holland, "The Laborers in the Vineyard."

31. Doctrine and Covenants 112:19.

32. "Early-Returned Missionaries Thrive with Acceptance, Love."

33. Ibid.

34. Olsen, "When a Missionary Returns Early."

35. Ibid.

36. "Early-Returned Missionaries Thrive with Acceptance, Love."

37. Ibid.

38. Doctrine and Covenants 64:29.

39. Lawrence Robinson, Melinda Smith, and Jeanne Segal, Emotional and Psychological Trauma: Symptoms, Treatments, and Recovery," *HelpGuide.org,* accessed March 9, 2016, http://www.helpguide.org/articles/ptsd-trauma/emotional-and-psychological -trauma.htm.

40. John 8:7.

41. John 8:9.

42. Doctrine and Covenants 18:13.

Don't pressure them. For returned missionaries, a lot of the problems they get are from stress, you know, from outside forces. Obviously, there are a lot of things we may need help on, but a lot of us have a purpose of what we want to do when we get back. We've been talked to by our mission presidents and we've been talked to by other people. When we get back, everyone tries to insert their own view. Sometimes, you need to lay off and let the returned missionaries make their own decisions.

> RETURNED MISSIONARY ELDER

Actually, it was not too bad at first coming home. I decided my first day I wanted to go do a lot of stuff and try to get a job and keep a schedule. That really helped me to kind of jump back into life. But at the same time, it was kind of hard because I wasn't used to normal life. It was also kind of weird being with a lot of people all the time, especially family members and I realized a lot of times they were always expecting to know what I was doing. As a missionary, we usually don't have to tell anyone what we are doing.

That was a little hard feeling like I had to tell someone what I was doing all the time. I would still try to fill my schedule full of things because as a missionary we would do that every day, but at the same time, because family members did not know that my schedule was always full, they would expect me to always do things with them. Of course, I want to see them as well, but I don't know their schedules either. It is always good to plan. I wish someone would say, "Hey, do you want to play tennis tomorrow?" If I knew ahead of time, then I could plan for it.

> RETURNED MISSIONARY ELDER

Handling Social Pressure

EVERYONE ELSE IS DOING IT!

It's great to be home!

While on your mission, your activities were very restricted. Now, all kinds of possibilities come back into your life. You can go to movies, you can play video games, and you can date.

You may feel a lot of pressure from family and friends to have fun, relax, and enjoy yourself. But, you may also feel a lot of pressure to do things you really don't want to do. Your friends might put pressure on you to play video games you don't feel comfortable playing anymore. Your parents may pressure you to date, but perhaps you just don't feel like you are ready. Your little brother may want you to watch all the superhero movies with him that you missed while you were gone, but you may find the violence of those movies really affects you negatively now. You may feel uncomfortable, but it seems like everyone else is doing it! If you don't, perhaps you'll feel like you're missing out or letting down your family and friends.

HOW DO YOU JUDGE?

The world is full of good, yet the world also has so much evil. How do you judge between these two parts of the world you now live in? How do you make the decisions to let certain activities back into your life and not to let others?

Moroni taught us the standard,

I show unto you the way to judge; for every thing which inviteth to do good, and to persuade to believe in Christ, is sent forth by the power and gift of Christ; wherefore ye may know with a perfect knowledge it is of God. But whatsoever thing persuadeth men to do evil, and believe not in Christ, and deny him, and serve not God, then ye may know with a perfect knowledge it is of the devil; for after this manner doth the devil work, for he persuadeth no man to do good, no, not one.[1]

While you were on your mission, you did try hard to only do things that "inviteth to do good." Now, many more choices and pressures are in front of you. As you work to have the Spirit with you, you will have the right to revelation to overcome these social pressures. Let the Spirit be your guide as you decide what you should do every day.

THE POWER OF THE DEVIL

As a returned missionary, Satan views you as having a large target painted on your chest. He wants to take you away from your eternal purpose and he will try his hardest using all of his worldly resources and worldly temptations. President Kimball said, "Lucifer desires all good people. . . . It seems that missionaries [and returned missionaries] are special targets."[2] You are a special target because you converted people to the truth and brought "people out of the dark where they are most vulnerable into the light where there is a measure of protection and where new strengths can be developed."[3] You are continuing to teach and influence people for good and Satan wants to stop you from doing that.

The power of the devil is limited by what power you give him in your life. The Prophet Joseph Smith taught, "The great principle of happiness consists in having a body. The devil has no body, and herein is his punishment. . . . All beings who have bodies have power over those who have not. **The devil has no power over us only as we permit him. The moment we revolt at anything which comes from God, the devil takes power.**"[4]

Because you have a body, the devil has no power over you unless you permit it. And as a returned missionary, you cannot rebel against anything that comes from God; otherwise, the devil will have power over you.

You can be spiritually confident that the devil will not have power over you as long as you stay on the Lord's side. President George Albert Smith taught, "There is a line of demarcation well defined between the Lord's territory and the devil's territory. If you will stay on the Lord's side of the line you will be under his influence and will have no desire to do wrong; but if you cross to the devil's side of that line one inch you are in the tempter's power and if he is successful, you will not be able to think or even reason properly because you will have lost the Spirit of the Lord."[5]

If you ask the Lord with a sincere heart and with real intent, you will know the answer to all of the questions you will face about whether to go to this or that activity or watch this or that movie. Sometimes, you may not want to know the answer, because the answer may mean not going with friends or family. But, asking with real intent means that you are willing to do whatever the Lord asks of you, even when His answer may be hard to accept.

BE A RIGHTEOUS EXAMPLE

You may find it hard to keep this high gospel standard. Sometimes, you may feel persecuted for the decisions you make. You're choosing to do the right and your friends are the ones having all the fun. It's just not fair!

Elder Joseph B. Wirthlin talked about a time he felt that life was unfair: "I remember one day after my football team lost a tough game, I came home feeling discouraged. My mother was there . . . 'Joseph,' she said, 'come what may, and love it.' . . . If we approach adversities wisely, our hardest times can be times of greatest growth, which in turn can lead toward times of greatest happiness."[6] Elder Wirthlin then described some ways that will help you deal with these times of adversity when you feel like life is not fair.

You can learn to laugh. "The next time you're tempted to groan, you might try to laugh instead. It will extend your life and make the lives of all those around you more enjoyable."[7] Making the choice to laugh about circumstances, rather than getting angry or frustrated, will also enable your family and friends to feel more at ease around you. They will not feel judged. The pressure of the situation will be lifted when you learn to laugh about it.

You can be grateful for the light and knowledge you have in your life. President Uchtdorf taught that being grateful will take the bitterness out of our life. He suggested that "instead of being thankful *for* things, we focus on being thankful *in* our circumstances—whatever they may be. . . . This is not a gratitude of the lips but of the soul. It is a gratitude that heals the heart and expands the mind."[8] Gratitude will help you seek for the eternal while finding joy in your righteous decisions, rather than finding hardship and pain.

As you become a happy and grateful example of righteous choices, others will follow you. Righteousness will be fun, rather than harsh and boring. King Benjamin has reminded you to "consider on the blessed and happy state of those that keep the commandments of God. For behold, they are blessed in all things, both temporal and spiritual; and if they hold out faithful to the end they are received into heaven, that thereby they may dwell with God in a state of never-ending happiness."[9]

ATTEND INSTITUTE

If you are having a difficult time finding friends who have the same standards and feelings about the gospel that you do, attend institute weekly. Not only will you enjoy great religious lessons, but you will also enjoy being with other people your age who want to learn about the gospel. President Thomas S. Monson invited you personally to attend institute and left you with a prophet's blessing if you do: "I ask you to make participation in institute a priority. . . . Friends will be made, the Spirit will be felt, and faith will be strengthened."[10] Institute is a great place to find new friends after your mission!

QUESTIONS OF THE SOUL

The doctrines of the Church are being attacked by many different social groups. Some of your friends may question your beliefs about certain social issues. Be an example of seeking for the truth in the right places. Be informed and make wise decisions as you study these issues and learn more about them. Seek well-documented sources and read statements by members and nonmembers alike about a variety of topics. As a citizen of your country and a member of Christ's Church, you should know where you stand on political and social issues.

You may have sincere personal or doctrinal questions that you want answered. The Church encourages us to ask soul-searching questions. The sincere question of a young teenage boy is what started the restoration of Christ's Church in these latter-days. Questions of the soul are encouraged, not discouraged, in our Church. President Uchtdorf said, "It's natural to have questions—the acorn of honest inquiry has often sprouted and matured into a great oak of understanding. There are few members of the

Church who, at one time or another, have not wrestled with serious or sensitive questions."[11]

As you have questions, start with what you know is true. The doubts you may have about certain gospel principles are part of learning and growing in the gospel. Be careful not to question *all* of your faith, because of a few doubts. Elder Holland offered this advice: "When problems come and questions arise, do not start your quest for faith by saying how much you do *not* have, leading as it were with your 'unbelief.' That is like trying to stuff a turkey through the beak! Let me be clear on this point: I am not asking you to pretend to have faith you do not have. I *am* asking you to be true to the faith you *do* have."[12] President Uchtdorf pleaded for you to "please, first doubt your doubts before you doubt your faith. [You] must never allow doubt to hold [you] prisoner and keep [you] from the divine love, peace, and gifts that come through faith in the Lord Jesus Christ."[13]

You may also want to reflect back on your mission and ask yourself:

- What did I do when my investigators had questions about the gospel?

- Where did I go to find answers to their questions?

On your mission, you learned the words of President Ezra Taft Benson when he said that the Book of Mormon "answers the great questions of the soul."[14] *Preach My Gospel* also teaches, "As we read the Book of Mormon with the guidance of the Spirit, it helps us answer personal questions."[15] You may want to seek your answers in the Book of Mormon, other scriptures, the words of our modern prophets, or personal prayer. These sources will help you find the right answers in a spiritual way.

AVOID DECEPTION

You may encounter social pressure from a friend who claims personal revelation as to what you should do in your life. Friends can also exhibit a great deal of emotion that will make you feel that they are sincere. President Howard W. Hunter offered this word of advice, "I think if we are not careful . . . , we may begin to try to counterfeit the true influence of the Spirit of the Lord by unworthy and manipulative means. . . . Certainly the Spirit of the Lord can bring strong emotional feelings, including tears, but that outward manifestation ought not to be confused with the presence of the Spirit itself."[16] You should pray for personal revelation and confirm your decisions with the teachings of modern prophets and the scriptures. Do not let your own emotions or the emotions of a dear friend cloud your decisions.

Robert Millett presented five questions you can ask yourself to determine if a person is trying to deceive you when they claim they've had a revelation concerning your life:

1. "Is the person claiming the revelation acting within the bounds of his or her respective stewardship?"

2. "Is the person receiving the revelation worthy to receive such?"

3. "Is the communication in harmony with the standard works and teachings of the prophets?"

4. "Does the revelation edify or instruct?"

5. "Does the communication build [your] faith and strengthen commitment?"[17]

The Lord taught the early saints ways to avoid deception. He said, "And this I give unto you that you may not be deceived, that you may know they are not of me. For verily I say unto you, that he that is ordained of me shall come in at the gate and be ordained as I have told you before, to teach those revelations which you have received and shall receive through him whom I have appointed."[18] You can avoid deception by following the prophet of God, whom God has appointed to receive revelation for His church. The prophets are always standing at the gate and know which way you should go.

To avoid personal deception, the Lord also admonished, "Wherefore, beware lest ye are deceived; and that ye may not be deceived seek ye earnestly the best gifts, always remembering for what they are given. . . . For all have not every gift given unto them; for there are many gifts, and to every man is given a gift by the Spirit of God."[19] Your spiritual gifts, especially the gift of the Holy Ghost, will help you also avoid deception. Rely on these gifts, rather than emotions, to make decisions in your life.

SOLVING PROBLEMS IN THE TEMPLE

Before your mission, you probably only had the opportunity of attending the temple a few times. Depending on where you served your mission, you may not have been able to attend a temple more than once a year or once a quarter, if at all. Even if your mission was blessed to have a temple nearby, you may have only been able to attend on special occasions, such as the sealing of one of your baptized members, or during a special mission-wide temple trip. These experiences would not have happened very often, even though they brought you great joy.

Now that you are home, you can choose to go to the temple as often as you want. You are not restricted concerning your temple attendance. The only challenge may be how far away the temple is from your home, or how difficult it is to get there. Most certainly, however, you will find hidden blessings and treasures of eternal knowledge as you make temple attendance a regular habit and a priority as you plan your life.

You may say to yourself, "How can I fit temple attendance into my busy schedule? I know it's important, but it takes three hours of my time. I just can't give up that kind of time."

How can you NOT fit temple attendance into your life? Attending the temple will enable you to understand God's plan for you now and free yourself from the relentless pressures of the world. President Howard W. Hunter said, "Let us be a temple-attending and a temple-loving people. Let us hasten to the temple . . . not only for our kindred dead, but let us also go for the personal blessing of temple worship."[20]

Jacob was working very hard after returning from his mission. He was trying to hold down two jobs in order to make enough money to go back to school in the fall. During this time, he started to attend institute regularly and was challenged to go to the temple at least once a week if his schedule would allow. He decided to make temple attendance a priority in his life and go the extra mile in this area of his life. He started going to the temple two times a week before or after work and once on Saturday. His testimony of the power of the temple grew in his life. Because of his regular temple attendance, he wanted to become a temple worker on Saturdays when he was not working. He talked to his bishop and was called by the temple presidency to work as an ordinance worker on a Saturday shift.

Even though Jacob's time in the temple did mean less time to play, he found his ability to handle his workload increased. His burdens seemed lighter and he could feel the refining influence of the temple in his life. He found temple work to be fun!

You may not be able to attend the temple as often as Jacob did or even on a weekly basis if you live far from the nearest temple, but you will find that the more frequently you attend, the more personal and powerful the blessing of temple worship will become. The temple is the best place for you to discover the solutions to problems and challenges in your life. When you have a problem and want to really think about it, the temple is a great place to figure out what the Lord wants you to know and to do about it.

Elder John A. Widstoe taught, "I believe that the busy person on the farm, in the shop, in the office, or in the household . . . can solve his problems better and more quickly in the house of the Lord than anywhere else. If he will leave his problems behind and in the temple work for himself and for his dead . . . a blessing will come to him, for at the most unexpected moments, in or out of the temple will come to him, as a revelation, the solution of the problems that vex his life. That is the gift that comes to those who enter the temple properly."[21] The temple is a place of revelation, peace, and safety from the world.

THE POWER OF THE SABBATH DAY

After your mission, you want to continue doing all the righteous things you did while on your mission and more. But, life happens! You may say to yourself, "Whoops, I really blew it this week! Now, what am I going to do?"

The power of the Sabbath day will enable you to go through a weekly refining and sanctification process. You can become purified once more, even after a really bad week, by prayerfully preparing to take the sacrament, repenting of your mistakes, and then partaking of the sacrament worthily.

Elder Don R. Clarke said, "If we have spent time before sacrament meeting repenting of our sins, we can leave sacrament meeting feeling clean and pure."[22] This is a process that will continue throughout your life. If every week, you will try to be a little better, a little better, and a little better, then, over time, you will be amazed at the improvements in your character, your actions, and your life.

Elder Boyd K. Packer explained the process: "The sacrament renews the process of forgiveness. Every Sunday when the sacrament is served, that is a ceremony to renew the process of forgiveness. . . . Every Sunday you cleanse yourself so that, in due time, when you die your spirit will be clean."[23]

The Lord commands you, "For verily this is a day appointed unto you to rest from your labors, and to pay thy devotions unto the Most High. . . . Thou shalt offer thine oblations and thy sacraments unto the

Most High, confessing thy sins unto thy brethren, and before the Lord."[24] The Lord promises that if you do this "the fulness of the earth is yours" and "he who doeth the works of righteousness shall receive his reward, even peace in this world, and eternal life in the world to come."[25]

There is real power in attending sacrament meeting, as well as all three hours of the Sunday block, and in keeping the Sabbath day holy— the entire day! You taught your investigators the importance of attending Church every Sunday. You taught them: "Our Sabbath-day behavior is a reflection of our commitment to honor and worship God. By keeping the Sabbath day holy, we show God our willingness to keep our covenants."[26] Now, you can show that same commitment to God each week and realize those same blessings in your life that you promised your investigators. Your Sabbath day attendance will help you handle all the social pressures you may encounter during the week and you will become "unspotted from the world."[27] That's the power of the Sabbath day in your life!

Suggestions for Parents

I'm not a completely different person, but my attitude has changed for the better. I still have the same likes and the same dislikes. When you first get home, I was warned that it would seem like your family is the worst sinners ever because you are used to having a strict schedule and standards. To be thrown into their normal [life], you ask yourself, "What am I going to do?" I need to remember that they are still my family. Having that love is the most important thing. Make sure you love them for who they are.

> RETURNED MISSIONARY ELDER

BE AN EXAMPLE OF THE BELIEVERS

Before leaving on the mission, your missionary felt more like your child than an adult. The mission has helped them to grow up very quickly. They are now adults. They will be looking to you as an example of what an adult living the gospel really looks like. They will be watching you more closely in the way you keep the Sabbath day holy, the way you pay your tithing and fast offerings, the way you treat other people on days other than Sunday, and the way you treat your family. They will be looking very closely at how they are supposed to act as adults now in their family and at church.

Paul counseled his friend, Timothy, "Be thou an example of the believers, in word, in conversation, in charity, in spirit, in faith, in purity. . . . Meditate upon these things; give thyself wholly to them."[28] As you, strive to be that kind of an example, you will "save thyself"[29] and save your returned missionary as well.

BE AN EXAMPLE OF TEMPLE SERVICE

Your returned missionary has not had the opportunity to make temple worship a regular habit in their life, yet. You need to be their example. Go regularly to the temple—weekly if a temple is nearby and if at all possible—and invite them to come along with you. Make it an open invitation and encourage them to make any sacrifices necessary to engage fully in temple service. Adult life is busy. Sometimes, temple service seems to get in the way of work and other adult responsibilities. Help your returned missionary figure out how to make the temple a part of their life as you share how you've made temple attendance a regular part of your life.

Personally, I have found that a major blessing of regular temple attendance is the gift of time. When I attend the temple regularly, I am able to see more clearly what I am supposed to do and accomplish in my life. Many years ago, I made the goal to attend the temple every week. I made this goal at the same time I was in a doctoral program, I had just had my twelfth child, three of my children decided to get married within a year of each other, and my husband, Steve, was the stake president. The temple kept my sanity, and brought peace into my life. I was inspired to know what the Lord would have me do during the week and how I could fit everything in by putting first things first.

The day I defended my dissertation, a woman came up to me and asked me how I did it. She explained that she was a member of the Church and had two children in school and did not know how she was going to take care of her home and family while doing her doctorate.

She asked me, "What is your secret? I want to know so I can do the same thing and finish my doctorate, too."

After thinking about it for a minute, I answered, "I go to the temple every week."

That was not the answer she was expecting to hear, but I knew if she followed my advice, it would help her find the time to accomplish what was most important to her and to the Lord.

When you put temple attendance foremost in your week, the Lord helps you prioritize your time and you are able to get so much more done. Regular temple attendance truly does enable you to use your time more wisely.

EACH RETURNED MISSIONARY
WILL NEED SOMETHING DIFFERENT

Being a parent is always a balancing act. You want to try to give your returned missionary support and encouragement, yet you do not want to become overbearing. You want them to rise up and become the adult you know they can become, yet you also want them still to remember that they are your child. The problem is that each returned missionary will need something different. Some returned missionaries still need direction and help to get started on adult life when they return home. Other returned missionaries just want you to get out of their way and let them get on with their adult life. You, as a parent, will need to be directed by the Spirit as to what role you need to play. If you have more than one returned missionary son or daughter, this role may change for each of these children.

Paul understood the importance of differences. He talked about righteous members of the church symbolically as the body of Christ with each member representing a different part of the human body (eye, ear, hand, foot, etc.). Each part has a different function and purpose, yet each part is necessary for the body to work properly: "For the body is not one member, but many. . . . The eye cannot say unto the hand, I have no need of thee: nor again the head to the feet, I have no need of you. Nay, much more those members of the body, which seem to be more feeble, are necessary."[30]

One of your returned missionaries may be a hand, very able and helpful; while another returned missionary may be a knee, always praying and seeking for inspiration; while another one may be an eye, constantly aware of others and what they are doing. Each of these returned missionaries will need your help in a different way.

Our son William came home to a different state, a different house, a different neighborhood, and a different ward. When he had packed his things before leaving on his mission, he had placed them in garbage bags. I thought they were garbage when we were moving, so I threw them all away. William had nothing familiar to come home to. He needed help

113

finding a doctor for a physical, finding a dentist to check his teeth, and shopping for new clothes (since he had none). All my other children had come back from their missions to a familiar place where they knew people and knew where things were. Understandably, William needed a lot more assistance than my other children. But others of our returned missionary children needed more emotional support, more love, more listening, or more gentle attention.

If you have a returned missionary who needs more help, be careful not to compare him or her with an older sibling. Carefully avoid making statements like the following:

- "Your brother John never needed me to do this for him when he came home."

- "Why is it taking you so long to get a job? Jessica had a job within a month of being home from her mission."

- "I don't understand why you need a break. Isaac started school the week he returned home from his mission."

When you make these comparisons, you are undermining their growth opportunity. You are labeling them as the younger sibling who cannot do anything right. Their different needs during their transition home from the mission may be just that—different.

DON'T BECOME DISCOURAGED

Some returned missionaries find the challenges of social pressure too much to handle. They either go back to old habits they had before or get involved with friends and activities that take them away from the spiritual person they have become on their mission.

Don't become discouraged, but continue forward with faith in Jesus Christ and His Atonement. Be patient with your son or daughter. Show forth an increase of love and support while never changing your gospel standards.

Alma the younger also had returned missionary sons. One son, Shiblon, had served faithfully and continued to serve in the church when he returned home. Alma said to Shiblon, "I have had great joy in thee already, because of thy faithfulness and thy diligence, and thy patience and thy long-suffering."[31] Another returned missionary son, Corianton, had made some wrong choices while on his mission and was struggling with his testimony now that he was home. These two returned missionaries were very different and had very different needs.

Alma gave Corianton beautiful and encouraging counsel in which he taught him about the Atonement and tried to explain very clearly about his opportunity to repent and change. His message was one of hope: "Therefore, my son, see that you are merciful unto your brethren; deal justly, judge righteously, and do good continually; and if ye do all these things then shall ye receive your reward; yea, ye shall have mercy restored unto you again; ye shall have justice restored unto you again; ye shall have a righteous judgment restored unto you again; and ye shall have good rewarded unto you again."[32]

Corianton did change his ways. He did return to the mission field "to preach the word unto this people"[33] and finally fulfilled a worthy mission.[34]

You can always have hope that your missionary will remember their mission and the good they have done. Give them the opportunity to start over if needed and always be there to support them and remind them (through your loving example) of the life they once led and the service they gave to the Lord.

NOTES

1. Moroni 7:16–17.
2. Spencer W. Kimball, *The Miracle of Forgiveness* (Salt Lake City, Utah: Bookcraft, 1969), 175.
3. Ibid.
4. Joseph Smith, *Teachings of the Prophet Joseph Smith,* comp. Joseph Fielding Smith (Salt Lake City, Utah: Deseret Book, 1976), 181; emphasis added.
5. *Teachings of the Presidents of the Church: George Albert Smith*, 2010, https://www.lds.org/manual/teachings-george-albert-smith/chapter-18?lang=eng.
6. Joseph B. Wirthlin, "Come What May, and Love It," *Ensign*, November 2008.
7. Ibid.
8. Dieter F. Uchtdorf, "Grateful in Any Circumstances," *Ensign, May* 2014.
9. Mosiah 2:41.
10. "Institute Quotes," *Institute of Religion*, institute.lds.org/about/quotes.
11. Dieter F. Uchtdorf, "Come, Join with Us," *Ensign*, November 2013.
12. Jeffrey R. Holland, "Lord, I Believe," *Ensign*, May 2013.
13. Uchtdorf, "Come, Join with Us."

14. Ezra Taft Benson. "Flooding the Earth with the Book of Mormon," *Ensign*, November 1988, 5.
15. *Preach My Gospel* (Salt Lake City, Utah: The Church of Jesus Christ of Latter-day Saints, 2004), 107.
16. Ibid., 99.
17. Ryan Morgenegg, "Five Ways to Detect and Avoid Doctrinal Deception," *Church News*, September 17, 2013, https://www.lds.org/church/news/five-ways-to-detect -and-avoid-doctrinal-deception.
18. Doctrine and Covenants 43:6–7.
19. Doctrine and Covenants 46:8, 11.
20. Howard W. Hunter, "First Presidency Message: The Great Symbol of our Membership," *Ensign*, October 1994, 5.
21. John A. Widtsoe, "Temple Worship," *The Utah Genealogical and Historical Magazine,* April 1921, 63–64.
22. Don R. Clarke, "Blessings of the Sacrament," *Ensign,* November 2012.
23. Boyd K. Packer, *Mine Errand from the Lord*, (Salt Lake City, Utah: Deseret Book, 2008), 196.
24. Doctrine and Covenants 59:10, 12.
25. Doctrine and Covenants 59:16, 23.
26. *Preach My Gospel*, 74
27. Doctrine and Covenants 59:9.
28. 1 Timothy 4:12, 15.
29. 1 Timothy 4:16.
30. 1 Corinthians 12:14, 21–22.
31. Alma 38:3.
32. Alma 41:14.
33. Alma 42:31.
34. See Alma 49:30.

There are a lot of social pressures, you know, to date, to talk to girls. And, it hasn't been easy. But I've adapted. For me, the whole social aspect hasn't been that difficult, honestly. When I left on my mission, I kind of cut off ties with most of my friends because my family moved to Utah, so there weren't many friends for me to come back to. So most of the friends I have now are all returned missionaries. I also have my family who are very supportive.

‣ RETURNED MISSIONARY ELDER

Well, that is one of the hardest things of coming home as a missionary— trying to jump into a social life again. You don't really have a social life as a missionary except your companion and your district. You are all there for the same purpose—so it is not a normal thing. But as soon as you get home there is a lot of pressure—like you need to go on a date the first day you get home— that kind of thing. And that is a little hard. I haven't talked to girls for two years. So I can't go on a date the same day I get home. . . . When I finally went out on a date, it was really cool. So I guess it is really fun to go out on dates and stuff. But you need to get back into it at your own pace.

‣ RETURNED MISSIONARY ELDER

Finding an
Eternal Companion

FINDING

While you were on your mission, how did you find people to teach? At first, it was probably very hard and awkward to make street contacts or to knock on doors; yet, you were able to overcome your initial reservations and do it. There were certainly days (and sometimes weeks or months) when you were having difficulty finding someone to teach. Yes, you probably made some contacts and taught a lesson or two here and there. You studied Chapter 9 of *Preach My Gospel* to receive ideas and inspiration. Often, you would need to work very hard to find the "golden" investigator who would really want to hear your message.

You will encounter many of the same kinds of challenges in your quest to find an eternal companion. Initially, you may need to overcome some initial reservations about meeting, dating, and conversing with others of the opposite sex. Finding the right person to date is hard work and you may experience times when you try to find the right person, yet all the people you meet are just passing contacts. Sometimes, you must be patient, yet always full of faith and hope that you will find that special someone.

A secret that most returned missionaries haven't discovered is that the principles and methods you practiced in finding someone to teach can be directly applied to finding a spouse! For example, *Preach My Gospel* taught you to talk to everyone. The following is a quote from *Preach My Gospel* with some wording changes: "Nothing happens in [courtship] until you find someone to [date]. Talk with as many people as you can each day. It is natural to be somewhat apprehensive about talking to people, but you can pray for the faith and strength to be more bold in opening your mouth."[1]

Some of the following missionary ideas from *Preach My Gospel* about how to talk with people can also be modified a bit to fit social and dating situations:

- Talk to people about their families and look for clues to help you begin talking with people of the opposite sex.

- Practice the listening skills you learned on your mission. Everyone likes to be listened to sincerely.

- Serving others and being warm, friendly, and cheerful will always open doors to get to know others in a deeper and more spiritual way.

- Seek help from the Spirit to help you know what to say.

- Ask friends and family members for the names of acquaintances who might be interested in dating you. [2]

This last point is effectively asking for "referrals" for someone to date. Sometimes, you may need a little extra support in order to go through with asking someone out. Having a friend set you up with someone they know or going on a double date makes it a little bit easier. Since friends and family know you so well, often they can refer someone they know who they feel will be a good match.

Don't be too quick to pass judgment on these suggestions. Remember on your mission how your best investigators were sometimes people who you initially thought would never want to hear the gospel. Be open to suggestions from family and friends without being judgmental.

The most important principle you learned about finding was to trust in the Spirit to help you find people to teach. Now, you must trust in the Spirit again, asking for help to know who you should date and where to find your eternal companion. Pray about it often and constantly ask for guidance in this most important decision in your life. *Preach My Gospel* taught you that "your efforts in finding will be effective if you are guided by the Spirit."[3]

LISTENING

As you talked to investigators, you would actively listen to them while they expressed their feelings about the things you were teaching. Even if they were just talking about their families, you would listen attentively, showing your interest in them personally.

You read about this teaching skill in Chapter 10 of *Preach My Gospel*: "When you listen carefully to others, you understand them better. When they know that their thoughts and feelings are important to you, they are more likely to be receptive to . . . share personal experiences, and make commitments."[4]

Other principles you learned as a missionary that can be helpful in your dating relationships now are not being afraid of silence, watching the communication of body language, and remembering that listening takes effort and concentration. These skills of active and reflective listening will help you in your communication and relationship with others, especially with your future spouse.

Elder Jeffrey R. Holland talked about the importance of listening in missionary work, but his points are also true in all of our relationships with others. "More important than speaking is listening. . . . Be genuine. Reach out sincerely. . . . If we listen with love, we won't need to wonder what to say. It will be given to us—by the Spirit."[5]

FOR THE STRENGTH OF YOU

While you were on your mission, you had a white handbook you carried around with you always. Our mission liked to play a game at zone conferences to see how well we all knew the Missionary Handbook. One person would begin reading a section out of the handbook and we would see who could be the first to find where that person was reading. Many missionaries became so proficient in their knowledge of that little book that all someone would need to read was just a few words and they knew where to find it.

Now that you are home, you do not have a white handbook that outlines everything you need to do. You do still have the scriptures and the words of the living prophets, though.

You may want to substitute your white handbook for a handbook with the Salt Lake Temple on the front and the words, "For the Strength of Youth." This booklet is the perfect handbook for you now. Cross out the "th" in "Youth" and it reads, "For the Strength of You." The First

Presidency Message in the front of the book has a promise for you if you follow these standards: "The standards in this booklet will help you with the important choices you are making now and will yet make in the future. We promise that as you keep the covenants you have made and these standards, you will be blessed with the companionship of the Holy Ghost, your faith and testimony will grow stronger, and you will enjoy increasing happiness."[6] Those are all promises you need right now in your life. The standards in this book were not only meant for you when you were a teenager, but also and especially while you are trying to find an eternal companion.

The only standards that no longer apply now that you are a returned missionary are that you can date one on one and you don't have to worry any more about steady dating with the same person.[7] In fact, you are now encouraged to date the same person frequently, especially if he or she is the right one.

Elder Dallin H. Oaks warned returned missionaries that they need to grow up when it comes to dating: "Men, if you have returned from your mission and you are still following the boy-girl patterns you were counseled to follow when you were fifteen, it is time for you to grow up. Gather your courage and look for someone to pair off with."[8] Elder Oaks also warned young women, "Young women, resist too much hanging out, and encourage dates that are simple, inexpensive, and frequent. Don't make it easy for young men to hang out in a setting where you women provide the food. Don't subsidize freeloaders." Elder Oaks's definition of a date incorporates the three Ps: (1) a date is **planned** ahead, (2) a date is **paid** for, and (3) a date includes being **paired** off with one other person.[9] Remember that dates do not need to be expensive and that creativity is always encouraged.

CHASTITY AND PROCREATION

Passion is a strong emotion. The Lord made us that way so that we want to procreate and have the blessings of family life. Experiencing these strong feelings is part of our human experience. In today's world, you will find growing promiscuity and an expectation that being unchaste is normal. The world teaches you to express your passion readily as a natural part of being human, rather than learning to control these feelings and explore them only in the bonds of marriage. Controlling your thoughts and feelings was an important part of your mission, and it is even more important now as you seek to find and marry your eternal companion worthily in the temple.

The standard for the world is to live together before marriage. In our mission, we once visited four lovely women investigators. Each one of them wanted to be baptized, but could not because they were not legally married to their "husbands." Their companions did not see the necessity of getting married. They said, "We have been together for many years. We don't need to pay the government all that money to be told we are married." Each of these women had tears in their eyes as they asked what they could do to soften the hearts of their companions. As a missionary, you probably experienced similar situations with people who were stuck between living in the world and wanting to live as a Latter-day Saint.

Now that you are home, do not let the philosophies of man and the bombardment of the world desensitize you or diminish your desire to remain chaste. Elder David A. Bednar said, "The doctrine [of chastity] will seem to be archaic and outdated to many people in a world that increasingly mocks the sanctity of procreation and minimizes the worth of human life. But the Lord's truth is not altered by fads, popularity, or public opinion polls."[10] Elder Robert D. Hales added this witness: "Standing obedient and strong on the doctrine of our God, we stand in holy places, for His doctrine is sacred and will not change."[11] The standard of chastity will not change. You must stand strong in the eternal standard of virtue without allowing the world's standards and lustful desires to change your path.

If you do find yourself in a position where you have allowed the influences of the world or the strong emotions associated with love to overpower your ability to choose the right, go to your bishop and repent. Remember the power of the Atonement you taught so forcefully on your mission as you strive to make yourself clean and worthy again.

NONNEGOTIABLE TRAITS

Elder Bruce R. McConkie's wise counsel was that "the most important single thing that any Latter-day Saint ever does in this world is to marry the right person in the right place by the right authority."[12] Your mission president probably made a statement very similar to that of Elder McConkie before you came home. Understanding your duty is much easier than doing it. Sometimes, the person you think is right for you doesn't feel the same way you do (and vice versa).

President Ezra Taft Benson talked specifically to young single adults about important principles to be following in finding an eternal companion. He taught, "Do not expect perfection in your choice of a mate. Do not be so particular that you overlook her most important qualities of having a strong testimony, living the principles of the gospel, loving home, wanting to be a mother in Zion, and supporting you in your priesthood responsibilities. Of course, she should be attractive to you, but do not just date one girl after another for the sole pleasure of dating without seeking the Lord's confirmation in your choice of your eternal companion."[13] Even though President Benson was specifically talking to men, the same council holds true for women, too. Don't be too picky about specific traits like hair color or body type, but make sure you are picky about testimony, worthiness, and Christlike attributes.

You should identify some nonnegotiable characteristics as you think about your future spouse. In our institute class for returned missionaries, we asked them to list the attributes they felt were necessary in their future eternal mate. Here are some of the nonnegotiable traits they listed:

- Has a testimony of the gospel of Jesus Christ
- The gospel is at the core of who they are
- Honest with self and others
- Has experienced true conversion
- Worthy to be sealed in the temple for time and all eternity
- Wants a family
- Respects and keeps covenants
- Constantly seeks to change for the better through the power of the Atonement
- Willing to sacrifice
- Completely faithful
- Kind to children
- Loves family and the Lord
- Works hard
- Has a good sense of humor

- Starts with the end in mind (has eternal goals and actions that reflect those goals)
- Strong interpersonal and problem-solving skills
- Humble
- Attends the temple regularly
- Understands Doctrine and Covenants 121
- Loves God more than he/she loves me
- Has a positive perspective on life
- Intelligent
- Completely trustworthy and my best friend
- Honors the priesthood/is a worthy priesthood holder
- Shows love and affection
- A good provider

You may want to write down the characteristics you feel are non-negotiable in your future spouse. Then, you will know what is most important to you as you try to find that special someone. Keeping these qualities in mind may make your search more focused and cause you to look at potential finding opportunities in a different way. As you do embark on your search, however, remember this counsel from Elder Hales: "None of us marry *perfection*; we marry *potential*. . . . Your responsibility now is to be worthy of the person you want to marry. If you want to marry a wholesome, attractive, honest, happy, hardworking, spiritual person, *be* that kind of person."[14]

THE DECISION TO MARRY

Many returned missionaries feel the pressure of finishing college and possibly graduate school, and then starting a job and buying a home before they get married. Many women would like to have a career before they decide to settle down and have children. All of these goals can get in the way of your goal to be married.

President Spencer W. Kimball told of the experience of meeting a returned missionary who was thirty-five years old and still had not married. When President Kimball asked him about it, he just laughed and showed little concern for his bachelorhood. President Kimball felt sorry for him and could only think about how he would be called upon at the Day of Judgment and asked about his wife. His answers to the Judge about being too busy working or getting an education or not being able to find the right girl would all sound hollow. As a prophet of the Lord, President Kimball pointed out, "He knew he was commanded to find a wife and marry her and make her happy. He knew it was his duty to become the father of children and provide a rich, full life for them as they grew up. He knew all this, yet postponed his responsibility."[15] Follow the advice of a prophet and don't postpone this eternal responsibility, especially if the Spirit prompts you that the opportunity has arrived. Elder M. Russell Ballard more recently confirmed this prophetic counsel when he stated: "The most important decision you will make in this life is the decision to marry the right [person] in the temple! While no one should rush this significant decision, all returned missionaries should be working on it."[16]

Don't let school or work get in your way of finding your eternal companion. Balancing work, school, and dating can be difficult, but if you keep in mind your eternal purpose, your understanding of why you are working or going to school will be put into the proper perspective.

John was having difficulty staying motivated to study and maintain his high grades while at the university. To motivate himself, he cut out pictures of random families in the Ensign magazine and put them on his school binder. He used these pictures to remind him of his eternal goal of having a celestial family someday. He did not want to lose sight of the real purpose of his university studies. As a result of this focus, he met and married a wonderful young woman (who was also a returned missionary) with whom he started a family and who also helped him complete his studies.

AN INVITATION

Finding your eternal companion is your next great journey of discovery. In order to help you on this journey, you may want to try the following activities:

1. When you go out on a date, try to find out something interesting or unique about the other person without specifically asking them, "What is something unique about you?" Ask meaningful and inspired questions to get to know them better. Follow the guidelines on asking effective

questions in Chapter 10 of *Preach My Gospel*. Then listen carefully to their answers. You will become a better listener through this activity and you will get to know your date on a deeper, more spiritual level as you ask the right questions and listen attentively.

2. Read the following five sections of *For the Strength of Youth*:

   - Dating
   - Dress and Appearance
   - Entertainment and Media
   - Music and Dancing
   - Sexual Purity

Determine if there is anything in your life that is not in accordance with these standards. If there is, then repent and change, just as you taught your investigators to do.

3. Review your own life currently in terms of how actively you are trying to find your eternal companion and how well you live the law of chastity. Ask yourself:

   - Am I willing to leave my comfort zone and put myself out into the social scene?
   - Are there things I should change in my relationships with others?
   - Am I living the law of chastity?

As you actively pursue finding an eternal companion, the Lord will bless your efforts. You will feel the Spirit of the Lord guiding you in your pursuits and you will feel at peace about this important part of your life as a returned missionary.

Suggestions for Parents

The only thing I can think of that was a concern for my son (and was also a concern for me) was his mission president telling him the same thing my mission president told me—to go home and get married. That is your number one responsibility to go home and get married quickly. He came home with a lot of pressure to find a wife. It is taking him about as long as it took me. I was twenty-seven when I found my wife and he is twenty-seven now and he has not found his wife. But I am in no hurry for him—because I want him to find the right one.

Maybe young men need that good pressure to find a wife. I think a wife turns a boy into a man. It is a responsibility he needs to receive.

All the young men and young women are different and receive criticism differently. I think you just need to be prayerful as a parent to know how much pressure is the right pressure. We are learning to become parents just like they are learning to become adults. We make mistakes. We just need to be prayerful. Be careful and do it with the Spirit.

> ▸ FATHER OF A RETURNED MISSIONARY

DON'T PRESSURE—SUPPORT AND ENCOURAGE

Returned missionaries often feel a lot of pressure from parents. There is a fine line between encouragement and pressure. Encouragement is a positive suggestion you give as a parent with the understanding that your son or daughter still can make their own decision and that you will not pressure them about it. When you pressure, you become dictatorial. You view your opinion as having more weight than your returned missionary's opinions. Acting this way will usually alienate them. They have been on their own for the last two years or eighteen months and have become used to making their own decisions. They have also become pretty good at it.

Sister Johnson knew who would make the perfect wife for her son, Tanner, when he returned home from his mission. Talley was a beautiful girl who was bright, played the piano, and was going to BYU. Sister Johnson had known her family for years. In fact, she was roommates with Talley's mother at BYU years ago. Sister Johnson tried to encourage her son to take Talley out on a date, but he felt uncomfortable with the arrangement. Then Sister Johnson started nagging him about "why" and "when." She kept asking him, "Why haven't you given Talley a call?" and "When are you going to take her out?" Every time her son went on a date with another girl, Sister Johnson would comment, "She's not as good as Talley!" Soon, her son stopped telling her about any of his dates altogether. The pressure he felt from his mother closed the door on any discussion they might have had about his love life.

Make sure that you stay on the side of encouragement, and do not cross over to pressuring! Encouragement is really what the father in the story above was talking about when he referred to the "right pressure." As with every other aspect of how you help your returned missionary, it is also essential that you be prayerful and guided by the Spirit regarding how much to encourage.

BE PATIENT

As a parent, we only want what is best for our child, no matter the age. We want them to be happy and fulfilled. Sometimes, our returned missionaries will not respond to our encouragement to marry and we may become frustrated. Sometimes, they have just not been able to find the right eternal companion, even though they are trying.

President Thomas S. Monson has counseled us; "Our problem is that we often expect instantaneous solutions to such challenges, forgetting that frequently the heavenly virtue of patience is required."[17] Paul taught, "But if we hope for that we see not, then do we with patience wait for it."[18] We hope for the eternal marriage of our children, but when we don't see it happening, we need to patiently wait for it to happen.

NOTES

1. *Preach My Gospel* (Salt Lake City, Utah: The Church of Jesus Christ of Latter-day Saints, 2004), 156–57.
2. Ibid., 156.
3. Ibid., 185
4. Jeffrey R. Holland, "Witnesses unto Me," *Ensign*, May 2001, 15.
5. *For the Strength of Youth*, "Message to the Youth from The First Presidency," ii.
6. *For the Strength of Youth*, "Dating," 4.
7. Dallin H. Oaks, "Dating versus Hanging Out," *Ensign*, June 2006
8. Ibid.
9. David A. Bednar, "We Believe in Being Chaste," *Ensign,* May 2013.
10. Robert D. Hales, "Stand Strong in Holy Places," *Ensign,* May 2013.
11. Bruce R. McConkie, "Choose An Eternal Companion," *Brigham Young University Speeches*, May 3, 1966 (Provo, Utah: Brigham Young University Press), 2.
12. Ezra Taft Benson, "To the Single Adult Brethren of the Church," *Ensign*, May 1988.
13. Robert D. Hales, "Meeting the Challenges of Today's World," *Ensign,* November 2015.
14. Spencer W. Kimball, "The Marriage Decision," *Ensign*, February 1975, 2.

Marianna & Steve Richardson

15. M. Russell Ballard, "Fathers and Sons: A Remarkable Relationship," *Ensign,* November 2009.
16. Thomas S. Monson, "Patience—A Heavenly Virtue," *Ensign*, November 1995, 59.
17. Romans 8:25.

One thing that is really difficult when you come home is the whole con-cept of constantly being active. You come home and everybody is like, "You need to take a break." It's kind of funny because there are two kinds of people when you get home from your mission: there are those who tell you to take a break, and there are those who tell you to keep the mind-set of the mission and continue to be active.

Sometimes, you feel kind of conflicted. Personally, I'm not going to say I've been perfect. I've definitely dabbled on both sides. There've been times as a returned missionary where I have just hung out and there have been times when I've been proactive and done stuff. Honestly, it's nice to have a break. But, in the end, I think the whole reason why you go on a mission is so that you can have that mind-set of being proactive. We go on a mission not only to change others, but to change ourselves. . . . So while taking a break is good, in the end, listening to those people who told me to continue being active in those things I did during the mission was much better.

    ▸ RETURNED MISSIONARY ELDER

Another challenge . . . was hard for me—in the mission, we get so much structure of schedule, and coming home we did not have that schedule any more. But you have your family that says, "Oh, just relax! Take some time. Take a semester off. Take a break from church." But I will encourage people to just get going, just jump right in. Get going on work, school; attend the temple; get busy and stay as active as you can. That's been a real strength for me.

    ▸ RETURNED MISSIONARY SISTER

Becoming Anxiously Engaged

The Lord commanded: "Verily I say, men should be anxiously engaged in a good cause, and do many things of their own free will, and bring to pass much righteousness."[1] After quoting this scripture, President Thomas S. Monson pointed out that our Savior should be our example as we contemplate what it means to be "anxiously engaged." President Monson said, "The sacred scriptures provide for you and me a model to follow when they declare, 'Jesus increased in wisdom and stature, and in favour with God and man.' And He 'went about doing good, . . . for God was with him.'"[2]

My Plan is a program that missionaries start when they receive their mission call and continue throughout their mission as they strive to be anxiously engaged in setting and achieving goals. Maybe you used *My Plan* while you were on your mission and your mission president reviewed your final goals during your last transfer. As you return home, you should review your goals with your stake president, your bishop, and your parents. If you did use *My Plan*, be sure to work toward the goals you set for yourself and continue to make plans for your future life.

CEASE TO BE IDLE

While you were on your mission, you found it easy to be anxiously engaged. Every minute of your day was scheduled and you only had one focus in your life—missionary work. You might ask yourself, as a full-time missionary:

- How much time did I spend serving the Lord each day?

- What acts of service did I perform?

- How did I show my commitment to the Lord?

You might ask yourself, as a returned missionary:

- How much time do I spend serving the Lord each day?

- What do I do with my discretionary time?

- How much time do I spend on Facebook, Twitter, or YouTube?

- What acts of service do I perform?

- How do I show my commitment to the Lord?

Being anxiously engaged can be a daunting task now that you are not serving the Lord full-time. Adult life is a constant balancing act between temporal and spiritual pursuits. With so much pressure, you may sometimes feel like doing nothing at all. But, President Monson has asked you to follow the example of the Lord and be anxiously engaged in a good cause. So, you must try.

The Lord taught the early saints some important principles about being anxiously engaged versus being idle:

- "Thou shalt not idle away thy time, neither shalt thou bury thy talent that it may not be known."[3]

- "Now, I, the Lord, am not well pleased with the inhabitants of Zion, for there are idlers among them; . . . they also seek not earnestly the riches of eternity, but their eyes are full of greediness."[4]

- "Behold, I say unto you that it is my will that you should go forth and not tarry, neither be idle but labor with your might."[5]

- "Let every man be diligent in all things. And the idler shall not have place in the church, except he repent and mend his ways."[6]

- "Cast away your idle thoughts and your excess of laughter far from you."[7]

- "Cease to be idle; cease to be unclean; cease to find fault one with another; cease to sleep longer than is needful; retire to thy bed early, that ye may not be weary; arise early, that your bodies and your minds may be invigorated."[8]

These are strong words from the Lord about the importance of not being idle and of keeping busy in His work. Usually, the first few days after you return home, all you want to do is sleep and relax. That's understandable. But after the first week or so, you need to get busy with your life and your future.

Blake had just returned home from his mission. He came home without a plan for his life. He didn't have a job nor had he signed up for school yet. He had been home long enough that he had seen everybody and done everything he wanted to do. He began to reminisce about his former missionary life and thought about the daily schedule. He missed waking up early, exercising, and reading his scriptures at the beginning of the day. He opened up his missionary planner, looked at the blank page on today's date, and wondered what he was going to do. He remembered planning with his companion and started thinking about what activities he could put in for each hour of the day to stay "anxiously engaged." He also wanted to start working toward some long-time goals and began to think about new key indicators he could work toward.

If you, like Blake, don't know what to do now, you may want to visit some of the following websites to help you get the direction you need.

To help you prepare a résumé, submit applications, and find a job, go to:

- www.ldsjobs.org

You may also want to look at the websites of companies you would like to work for and start filling out job applications on those sites.

For Church school applications and help on how to pay for school or how to choose a major, as well as for other information on schooling, visit these websites:

- www.besmart.com
- www.mynextmove.org

Here are only a few of the many websites that will help you identify and apply for scholarships and financial aid:

- www.finaid.org
- www.fafsa.ed.gov
- www.collegeboard.com
- www.fastweb.com
- www.cashforcollege.com

Please understand that you can often earn more money per hour spent applying for scholarships than you could ever earn per hour working. This is not to say that you shouldn't work to earn money for school, but rather that you should be sure to take advantage of the huge number of scholarships and grants available to potential students from all walks of life and circumstances.

You may also want to talk to a counselor at a local university or an advisor at one of the many LDS employment centers to get help on school and work possibilities. After observing the experiences of many returned missionaries, we strongly recommend the Career Workshop offered at LDS employment centers.

SET GOALS!

In *Preach My Gospel*, you were taught as a missionary, "Goals reflect the desires of our hearts and our vision of what we can accomplish. Through goals and plans, our hopes are transformed into action. Goal setting and planning are acts of faith. Prayerfully set goals that are in harmony with the Savior's command[s]."[9] Gaining the vision of what you are supposed to accomplish may take time. The Spirit will guide you as you move forward. Sometimes, you may need to take one step into the darkness, but soon, your path will become clear.

Elder M. Russell Ballard taught, "I am so thoroughly convinced that if we don't set goals in our life and learn how to master the techniques of living to reach our goals, we can reach a ripe old age and look back on our life only to see that we reached but a small part of our full potential. When one learns to master the principles of setting a goal, he will then be able to make a great difference in the results he attains in this life."[10]

The Lord has great things planned for your life. If you let him guide you, you will be amazed and surprised at the places He will take you. President Uchtdorf told the story of a man who had always wanted to enjoy the sites of Europe. He saved up all of his money to go on an ocean cruise. He would have liked to enjoy the food and the entertainment on the ship, but he was worried about having enough money. Instead, he lived on stale crackers, canned goods, and powdered drinks. At the end of his journey, he found out that all the food and entertainment were included in the price he paid for the cruise. He could have enjoyed it all if he had only asked and sought out his opportunities. President Uchtdorf observed, "We are faced with a choice. We can be satisfied with a diminished experience . . . and settle for experiences far below our privileges. Or we can partake of an abundant feast of spiritual opportunity and universal priesthood blessings."[11]

In order to participate in this feast of opportunity, you must ask, plan, and work for it. You will need to establish some new key indicators to help you reach the longer term goals you have in your new life. Here are some suggestions for key indicators you may want to establish (there are many others, depending on your long-term goals and preferences):

- Time spent per day studying the scriptures
- Time spent per day or week exercising
- Number of kneeling prayers per day
- Number of dates or social activities per week
- Number of temple ordinances performed per week or month
- Number of ancestor names submitted for temple work per week or month
- Number of ward missionary or home/visiting teaching visits per week
- Number of contacts made or referrals submitted per week
- Number of résumés or job applications submitted per week
- Number of acts of service per day or week
- Time spent doing homework per day
- Grades earned or classes taken per semester

With your planner (or smartphone), you can make and track daily, weekly, or monthly goals for these new key indicators, evaluating them on a regular basis, just as you did on your mission. This will require regular planning, of course. One plan may not be enough to accomplish all these things. Life often gets in the way. You may need to set up a Plan A, Plan B, and Plan C to make sure you achieve your goals for these key indicators, just like the backup plans you made on the mission. Remember to start your planning with prayer and ponder how you will accomplish your goals. You will be surprised by how much you will be able to accomplish as you follow the same procedure you followed on your mission of setting goals during weekly and daily planning.

GO ABOUT DOING GOOD

Becoming anxiously engaged is not just about improving yourself, but you must also be looking for ways to help others. Elder Ballard described how bees all work together to accomplish the work of the hive. In this same way, our "simple, daily acts of service may not seem like much in and of themselves, but when considered collectively they become just like the one-twelfth teaspoon of honey contributed by a single bee to the hive. There is power in our love for God and for His children, and when that love is tangibly manifest in millions of acts of Christian kindness, it will sweeten and nourish the world with the life-sustaining nectar of faith, hope, and charity."[12] Elder Ballard asked us to pray each morning to find one person who we can serve or for whom we can perform a simple act of kindness. As you go to work or school, have your heart filled with charity and love for others and be looking for ways to fulfill this daily goal.

In *Preach My Gospel*, you were taught the same principle in the section, "Go About Doing Good." You can have the faith to find people to serve, just like you had faith to find people while you were on your mission. This kind of service is unplanned, but "involves listening to the Spirit to recognize opportunities for small, simple acts of kindness that you can offer to God's children."[13]

BE A LIVELY MEMBER

Your Sunday experience may be very different now that you are a returned missionary. As a full-time missionary, you would enter the chapel and everyone would be shaking your hand and looking for you. You would have meetings and things to do all day. However, after the first few Sundays home, you may not have anyone who comes up to talk to you spontaneously. You may not have a Church calling and you may not feel as wanted or needed as you did on your mission. But you are needed!

There are many activities you can be anxiously engaged in, especially on Sundays.

The Lord admonished Frederick G. Williams to be a "lively member."[14] What a great phrase! You can be a lively member as you seek for ways to serve in your ward each Sunday, without being asked. You can be a lively member by asking your bishop, elders' quorum president, or Relief Society president about ward members who need a visit or some special service.

Here are some additional ideas to help improve your Sunday experience and that of others:

- Participate fully in class discussions and Sunday activities.

- Prepare for Sunday School and Priesthood or Relief Society by reading and studying the assigned lessons during the week.

- Take notes during sacrament meeting talks and classes, specifically recording the points the Spirit whispers are most important for you.

- Fellowship new, less-active, or shy members, and of course, nonmembers, during meetings. Actively seek out those to sit next to, and talk to them and make them feel welcome. Become a friend to someone who needs a friend.

- Become a self-appointed greeter in the foyer or in class. This includes strengthening those who look like they may have had a difficult week.

- Help with the setup and cleanup of chairs, tables, classrooms, etc. Go around the chapel and pick up garbage, straighten hymnbooks, etc.

- Prepare yourself to partake the sacrament worthily and to focus on the Atonement during the sacrament portion of the meeting.

As you seek for opportunities to serve, they will find you! You taught your new converts, "It is not enough for people to simply come into the Church. They must come to stay. . . . In order to receive all the blessings that our Heavenly Father has in store for them, members must continue to live the gospel and be active in the Church."[15] You will become anxiously engaged in the work of the Lord as you continue to be a "lively member" who actively seeks for the Lord's help in accomplishing your goals, doing good to others, and fully participating in your Church meetings and activities.

Suggestions for Parents

I think one of the worst things you can do is plan a vacation the week he comes home—because it is too much free time. He's been programmed eighteen hours a day and you're saying, "You have nothing to do. We're just going to hang out together." He doesn't need time to hang out. He needs time to serve others. That's what he is used to doing. What's better? Hanging out or serving someone else? Go down to [a welfare center] and work if you need to find someplace. Go to a preschool and work. But don't just hang out.

> ❯ MOTHER OF A RETURNED MISSIONARY

The best advice I'd heard was "Get busy!" Not just studying scriptures all day every day, but get busy. Get a job. Try to transition into school quickly at the half semester. Just get busy and that will help you start new habits and help you in your transition.

> ❯ FATHER OF A RETURNED MISSIONARY

BE AN EXAMPLE, NOT A CRITIC

President Thomas S. Monson has advised us, "Fathers, grandfathers, we have an even greater responsibility to guide our precious sons and grandsons. They need our help, they need our encouragement, they need our example. It has been wisely said that our youth need fewer critics and more models to follow."[16] As you contemplate your role as parents to your returned missionary, think about the model of behavior you are portraying to them, rather than just criticizing their behavior. You may want to ask yourself if you are always anxiously engaged in a good cause. If you are not, you may want to review your own life and contemplate ways to improve.

ENCOURAGE THEM TO ATTEND ONE WARD

When missionaries first return home, they want to visit their old friends. Many of their friends will be returning from their missions at the same time they are and they will want to attend their sacrament meeting talks as they come home. Sundays could become a time for ward hopping, going from ward to ward to visit friends and relatives rather than attending one ward each Sunday. Strongly encourage them to pick one ward to attend regularly and to receive a calling in that ward as soon as possible, even if they want to attend other sacrament meetings with their friends in addition to their own.

Your missionary can decide if he or she would like to attend your home ward or attend a young single adult ward. In the handbook of instructions, young single adults are advised to consult with their parents about which ward they should attend: "Eligible members may, **in consultation with their parents**, choose to be members of the young single adult ward or to remain in their conventional ward."[17] Your returned missionary might want to discuss this also with ward leaders in each ward to find out where they could be the greatest help. If you have a conventional ward that needs support, especially with prospective missionaries or missionary work, a returned missionary could be a great help for the members of that ward.

LOVINGLY HELP THEM TO BECOME FUNCTIONING ADULTS

Finding a job is hard work. Your returned missionary may need some advice from you on how to write a résumé, how to dress for a job interview, how to respond in a job interview, and how to apply for jobs. If they are planning to go to school, they may need help finding scholarship money or applying for schools. If you are unable to help them in these areas, then direct them to resources in your community where they can find help. The Church has many resources as well, especially LDS Employment Centers, which can support them in this important work of determining what to do in their life now.

Encourage them to fast and pray about their future. You may want to fast with them, too. If they need a priesthood blessing, give them a blessing or help them receive one, so they can feel the direction of the Lord in their lives.

NOTES

1. Doctrine and Covenants 58:27.
2. Thomas S. Monson, "Anxiously Engaged," *Ensign*, November 2004.
3. Doctrine and Covenants 60:13.

4. Doctrine and Covenants 68:31.

5. Doctrine and Covenants 75:3.

6. Doctrine and Covenants 75:29.

7. Doctrine and Covenants 88:69.

8. Doctrine and Covenants 88:124.

9. *Preach My Gospel* (Salt Lake City, Utah: The Church of Jesus Christ of Latter-day Saints, 2004), 146.

10. Ibid., 146.

11. Dieter F. Uchtdorf, "Your Potential, Your Privilege," *Ensign,* May 2011.

12. M. Russell Ballard, "Be Anxiously Engaged," *Ensign,* November 2012.

13. *Preach My Gospel*, 168.

14. Doctrine and Covenants 92:2.

15. *Preach My Gospel*, 221.

16. Thomas S. Monson, "Anxiously Engaged," *Ensign,* November 2004.

17. *Handbook 2: Administering the Church*, "16.4 Young Single Adult Wards"; emphasis added.

The best way to cope with coming home is to keep doing what you are supposed to be doing—keep reading the scriptures, praying, going to Church, and being encouraging—just like when you were on your mission. That's the best thing for us.

› RETURNED MISSIONARY SISTER

Hastening the Work as a Seasoned Warrior

As a missionary, you envisioned yourself as a soldier in the army of Helaman sent out to bring the world His truth. Now that you are home, you are a seasoned warrior—the vanguard to teach the younger and less experienced striplings in the army of Helaman. Your new responsibility is to be an example to young and old alike of the principles you learned on your mission.

THE IMMORTALS

The ancient Persian army under King Cyrus, King Darius, and King Xerxes had a special elite troop of ten thousand warriors. Herodotus described them as *the Immortals*. They were known for their strength and courage in battle. They displayed great courage during the Battle of Thermopylae against the Spartans in 479 BCE. While the rest of the Greeks blocked a narrow road along the coast of Greece preventing the Persians from invading, the Immortals made a detour and attacked the Greeks from the rear.[1] Herodotus wrote: "This corps was known as the Immortals, because it was invariably kept up to strength; if a man was killed or fell sick, the vacancy he left was at once filled, so that its strength was never more nor less than ten thousand."[2]

You, as returned missionaries, are like this advanced guard of elite troops. The main difference between you and the Immortals is that the Church does not want to lose a single one of you seasoned warriors. Another difference is that instead of the number of warriors in this elite group remaining constant battle after battle, the number is growing larger and larger as more and more missionaries return home to help hasten the work.

THE ARMIES OF ANTIPUS, GID, AND TEANCUM

The army of Helaman was not alone in their battles. They had other Nephite armies who helped and supported them. These experienced warriors fought alongside the younger, more inexperienced ones. Helaman took his striplings to assist Antipus and his warriors, who were trying to maintain the city of Judea against the Lamanite armies. Antipus's army had suffered much and were "depressed in body as well as in spirit"[3] to the point that they had "determined to conquer in this place or die."[4] Antipus and Helaman's armies joined together in the fight. The sheer numbers of Helaman's young band were enough to stop the Lamanite armies from attacking them when they first arrived. The fathers of the stripling warriors brought provisions, which strengthened the entire army. The army of Antipus revived and became much stronger with the support of the younger army.

Similarly, you, our army of returned missionaries, are experienced and well-trained, and can join forces with our army of currently serving missionaries. Missionaries and returned missionaries can bolster and strengthen each other in building up the kingdom of God throughout the world.

After their victory in the city of Judea, the army of Helaman joined with the armies of Antipus and Gid to obtain the city of Cumeni. The Lamanites were starving in this city because no food nor provisions could get through to them, and they eventually yielded the city to the Nephite army. The Nephites now had a problem; the Lamanite prisoners were too numerous for them to guard and to feed. They had to use all their manpower to guard the prisoners and they had barely enough food and supplies for their own people, let alone all these extra mouths to feed. Gid and his army were chosen to guard the prisoners down to the land of Zarahemla. The day they left, a numerous Lamanite army with provisions was sent by King Ammoron to attempt to retake Cumeni. This fresh army battled the remainder of the Nephite armies, including the stripling warriors, who were stationed there.

The battle was fierce. The Lamanites were on the verge of victory when Gid and his army returned in the nick of time. Helaman attributed the Nephite victory in this battle to Gid's army and to the two thousand and sixty stripling warriors, who beat the Lamanites and drove them back to the city of Manti. This victory was only realized because the army of Gid returned and supported the younger army. You returned missionaries can provide sustaining power and influence to our younger missionaries in the same way.

HASTENING THE WORK

The Church has recently focused with great intensity on hastening the work and preparing elders and sisters to go forth and serve as missionaries. Our missionary force has grown dramatically since the announcement of the age change for young men and women who desire to serve as full-time missionaries.[5] In October 2012, the number of full-time missionaries was 58,500. That number increased to over 88,000 in October 2014. Many of you reading this book have been part of this wonderful flood of missionaries who are now returning home. You are an army of prepared and obedient young men and women who went out into the world to share the gospel of Jesus Christ and have come home excited about your new assignment to continue serving. You are now willing to work hard and serve the Lord, not just for two years or eighteen months, but for the rest of your lives and eternity.

You are the lifeblood of the movement to hasten the work because you understand the necessity for every member to find people for the missionaries to teach and to invite to come unto Christ. You know that members must leave their comfort zone and push a little harder to share the gospel in their neighborhoods and workplace. You did exactly this for two years or eighteen months and you know how to do it well. You are the examples that the rest of the Church will follow.

ARE YOU A SUCCESSFUL RETURNED MISSIONARY?

Many missionaries ask themselves, their companions, and their mission presidents while they are on their mission, "How can I know if I am a successful missionary?" Too often, missionaries think this answer has to do with their key indicators and, in particular, how many baptisms they had during their mission.

Now you may be asking yourself a very similar question: "How can I know if I am a successful returned missionary?" The answer for both of these questions is found on pages 10 and 11 of *Preach My Gospel:*

"You can know you have been a successful [returned] missionary when you:

- Feel the Spirit testify to people through you.

- Love people and desire their salvation.

- Obey with exactness [the commandments of God].

- Live so that you can receive and know how to follow the Spirit, who will show you where to go, what to do, and what to say.

- Develop Christlike attributes.

- Work effectively every day, do your very best to bring souls to Christ, and seek earnestly to learn and improve.

- Help build up the Church (the ward) wherever you [live].

- Warn people of the consequences of sin. Invite them to make and keep commitments.

- Teach and serve other[s].

- Go about doing good and serving people at every opportunity."[6]

This is an excellent list to review often in your life. Your regular self-evaluation will focus your efforts as you move forward and will help you understand your purpose better.

Elder Holland told the story of being a young father leaving Utah with his wife and small children to go to graduate school back East. His car died on the highway before he had gone forty miles. He thought he had fixed it and had started the journey again when his car died a second time in exactly the same spot. Decades later, he was driving that same stretch of highway and imagined that he saw himself—that same young, worried, and desperate father—walking for help along the side of the road. Elder Holland described the moment: "In that imaginary instant, I couldn't help calling out to him: 'Don't you quit. You keep walking. You keep trying. There is help and happiness ahead.' Some blessings come soon, some come late, and some don't come until heaven. But for those who embrace the gospel of Jesus Christ, *they come*. It will be all right in the end. Trust God and believe in good things to come."[7]

All of the skills and lessons you learned on your mission can and should be practiced in your current life. Your mission was really only a boot camp for your real life's mission ahead. As you continue to strengthen your ward and family, to serve in your Church callings, to keep the commandments, to do family history work and attend the temple often, and to be an active member missionary, you will experience even greater joy and spiritual satisfaction than you did on your mission. Your mission will not be the best two years of your life, but only the beginning of greater things to come!

Suggestions for Parents

My youngest son was very anxious about what he should do when he came home. So I challenged him to get up every morning at 5:30 a.m. and watch the BYU Devotionals and then a conference talk and read his scriptures. So he started his day that way. He transitioned into a good sleep pattern very quickly, too.

> ‣ MOTHER OF A RETURNED MISSIONARY

AS PARENTS, KEEP YOUR COVENANTS

The parents of the striplings in the army of Helaman were the inspiration and guides for their sons who became the stalwart hero–warriors of the Book of Mormon. Their fathers had covenanted never to take up arms against another person again. That covenant was something they were unwilling to break, until they witnessed the suffering of the Nephites who were protecting them and their families. Then, "they were moved with compassion and were desirous to take up arms in the defence of their country."[8] They came very close to breaking their covenant with the Lord because of the "dangerous circumstances at this time."[9] But, Helaman successfully persuaded them to abandon this course of action. He "feared lest by so doing they should lose their souls."[10] Their covenant was eternally binding and he knew they must not risk their eternal salvation.

Their sons followed the example of their fathers and "entered into a covenant to fight for the liberty of the Nephites."[11] These young men knew how to be covenant keepers because of the example of their fathers. They entered into a binding and eternal covenant on their own accord because they had seen their fathers do so. The strength and power of these young warriors came from their commitment to keep their covenants.

The mothers of these young men are also celebrated because they instilled a strong and abiding faith in their sons regarding the promises the Lord had given them. Their mothers taught them the gospel of Jesus

149

Christ and how to be the kind of men that were "exceedingly valiant for courage" and "true at all times in whatsoever thing they were entrusted."[12] They were men of "truth and soberness, for they had been taught to keep the commandments of God and to walk uprightly before him."[13]

Helaman led his stripling warriors to assist the struggling Nephite armies against a numerous Lamanite host. Before their first battle, Helaman asked these young men who had never fought before: "Therefore what say ye, my sons, will ye go against them to battle?"[14] Their answer inspired Helaman as it illuminated their simple but unshakable faith: "Father, behold our God is with us, and he will not suffer that we should fall; then let us go forth."[15] Helaman asked them further, how they could be so bold, when they were unseasoned concerning the rigors and terrors of battle. These young men rehearsed the words of their mothers "that if they did not doubt, God would deliver them."[16] They went even further to say, "We do not doubt our mothers knew it."[17]

Parents today need to teach their children, even their returned missionaries, these same principles by precept and by example. Fathers need to be unwavering in their determination to keep sacred covenants no matter the circumstance or the difficulties that befall them. Mothers need to teach their children the gospel of Jesus Christ and instill within them the conviction that they will be saved through their faithfulness, even while the terrors of battle against sin and destruction rage around them. Mothers need to be the champions of eternal families and examples of true motherhood to their sons and daughters as well as to all others.

BINDING UP WOUNDS AND STRENGTHENING OUR WARRIORS

The army of Helaman fought alongside the armies of the Nephites to maintain the city of Cumeni. Their families had already played an important part in strengthening them while they were in battle. Earlier, the additional sixty warriors had come from their homes, providing them with new strength and needed food and supplies as they joined their ranks.[18] After the battle was over, their families continued to play an important part, especially in helping the young men heal from the wounds of battle.

We are told that 200 of the 2,060 warriors had fainted because of the loss of blood and "there was not one soul . . . among them who had not received many wounds."[19] In order to keep fighting, they needed to have their wounds bound up and to get their strength back before they could fight again.

After the battle, we can imagine the mothers of these young men coming to them and binding up their wounds, preparing them to return to battle. Some of them were probably too hurt to return to the battlefield. They needed to return home to heal and have their wounds tended by professional healers. Those who had to return home early were still acclaimed as valiant warriors, acknowledged for their bravery and courage.

Our returned missionaries, both those who come home early and those who serve for the entire period of their call, may also need their wounds to be cared for and bound up with the help of professional healers, family, and friends. Each returned missionary's needs are unique, similar to the varying but unique needs of the wounded stripling warriors. Situations are different and missionaries will need to be watched over with care and under the direction of the Spirit before returning to missionary service, or to work or school.

KEEPING OUR RETURNED MISSIONARIES SAFE

While your missionary was serving, you prayed intensely every day for their safety and welfare. You wrote them letters every week. Do you still pray for them every day? Do you still communicate with them with the same intensity and longing? If not, you may consider ways you can communicate better with them and with the Lord in their behalf.

Even with all of the existing efforts to support our returned missionaries, we are losing too many of them. Many of them find themselves feeling unneeded. The knowledge, testimony, and skills they acquired as missionaries are often wasted as they find themselves without helpful guidance or opportunities to serve. They need assistance during their transition home and they need opportunities to still feel needed and valued.

The direction and example parents can provide is crucial to the success of these returning warriors. They need to keep on their armor of God and be ready for battles they will now face. They must not falter, but remain ever prepared to help themselves and others in the great hastening of the work of salvation.

The hymn, "Behold! A Royal Army," describes our returned missionaries well:

Behold! A royal army, with banner, sword, and shield,

Is marching forth to conquer on life's great battlefield.
Its ranks are filled with soldiers, united, bold, and strong,
Who follow their Commander and sing their joyful song.[20]

It is our duty and blessing as parents to be their example and guide as they victoriously return home. The Lord has promised them and us: "And inasmuch as ye are humble and faithful and call upon my name, behold, I will give you the victory."[21] Let us, together with our returned missionaries, joyfully sing "Victory, victory, thru Jesus Christ, our Lord!"[22]

NOTES

1. Jona Lendering, "Immortals," *Livius*, last modified July 27, 2015, http://www.livius.org/articles/concept/immortals/.
2. Pierre Briant, *From Cyrus to Alexander: A History of the Persian Empire*, trans. Peter T. Daniels (Winona Lake, Indiana: Eisenbrauns, 2002), 261.
3. Alma 56:16.
4. Alma 56:17.
5. Thomas S. Monson, "Welcome to Conference," *Ensign,* November 2014.
6. *Preach My Gospel* (Salt Lake City, Utah: The Church of Jesus Christ of Latter-day Saints, 2004), 10–11.
7. Jeffrey R. Holland, "Good Things to Come," Sharing the Gospel Online, https://www.lds.org/church/good-things-to-come?lang=eng.
8. Alma 53:13.
9. Alma 53:15.
10. Ibid.
11. Alma 53:17.
12. Alma 53:20.
13. Alma 53:21.
14. Alma 56:44.
15. Alma 56:46.
16. Alma 56:47.
17. Alma 56:48.
18. Alma 57:6.
19. Alma 57:25.
20. Fanny J. Crosby, "Behold! A Royal Army," *Hymnal* (Salt Lake City, Utah: The Church of Jesus Christ of Latter-day Saints, 1985), 251.
21. Doctrine and Covenants 104:82.
22. Crosby, "Behold! A Royal Army."

For Parents of
Future Missionaries

Parents often comment, "I wish I had known this before I sent out my first missionary." We feel the same way! We are still learning what to do and what not to do with our returned missionaries and how to better prepare our youngest children and grandchildren for the great full-time missionary adventure. Elder Richard G. Scott reminded parents that the process of preparation "begins in the home long before missionary age when parents instill in the minds and hearts of every young boy the concept of 'when I go on a mission,' not 'if I go on a mission.'"[1] Similarly, Elder David A. Bednar taught us, "The single most important thing you can do to prepare for a call to serve is to *become* a missionary long before you go on a mission."[2]

Our future missionaries need to have the skills necessary to feel like they can live on their own without the constant supervision of their parents. As parents, we need to help our children become self-reliant and self-confident to handle the challenges of missionary service in other parts of the country and the world. Here are some suggestions for your younger children as they prepare emotionally, physically, socially, and spiritually to become full-time missionaries.

EMOTIONAL PREPARATION

Always support and love your children, but teach them to take care of their own problems if they can. Give them the tools and understanding to deal with everyday situations. Do not do everything for them. If a problem comes up, let them try to fix it while giving them the support and love they need to be successful.

The following are some examples of activities you can teach your future missionaries to do, especially during that crucial final year of preparation:

- Encourage your future missionaries to communicate any emotional problems they may be having, *before* these problems become too difficult for them to handle. Communication is a crucial key for missionaries to learn in order to manage emotional problems successfully. If they feel they need to hide such problems or can't talk about them, then they may experience problems on the mission that will result in an early return. Help them not to feel embarrassed or ashamed because they may struggle emotionally. Teach them that feelings of depression and frustration are often very normal on a mission and need to be discussed openly with priesthood leaders.

- Teach and trust them to go to the store on their own. Give them a budget for food and let them prepare meals for the family. These experiences will increase their self-confidence and their ability to accomplish these same tasks on their mission successfully without feeling tense and worried.

- Teach them to make an appointment for the dentist or the doctor on their own. Let them make the appointment for their missionary physical and dental office visits. Teach them how to manage their own bank account. If they are under eighteen years old, you will need to go to the bank initially to help them set up an account. Follow-up, but let them be as self-reliant as possible.

- Teach them to clean up after themselves. Have them be responsible for their room, the kitchen dishes, the laundry, the yard, and other areas of your home. A clean living environment during their mission will affect them emotionally in a positive way.

For all of these points, you may want to have family home evening lessons and then follow-up to make sure your prospective missionaries feel comfortable with their emotional preparation for their mission.

If your son or daughter is currently on medication for emotional or neurological issues, please be completely truthful about this on their missionary application. The most important way they (and you) can prepare for their missionary service in this situation is to demonstrate that they have been stable on their medications over a prolonged period of time (a year or more). It is absolutely essential that they continue taking them and do not stop before or during their mission. The information in their application about the medications they are taking will be very helpful for missionary placement and for their future mission president to know how to support them effectively.

A missionary can serve a very successful mission while taking such medications. This fact will not necessarily restrict their service to certain areas or countries—this is a common yet unjustified concern of some prospective missionaries and their parents. The Lord will still send missionaries where they are supposed to serve.

PHYSICAL PREPARATION

You may want to use this time of preparation to evaluate your family's eating and exercise habits. This evaluation will not only help your missionary, but your entire family's physical health.

Here are some suggestions:

- As a family, encourage regular exercise. Instead of going to a movie, go outside and play a friendly game of football, basketball, or softball. Encourage your children to be active. After spending the day sitting at school, discourage them from coming home just to sit in front of a computer and a television each day. The habit of regular exercise will also foster better emotional health and self-esteem, as your future missionaries begin to look better and feel better.

- Train and encourage your future missionaries to understand good nutrition. Help them realize the importance of vegetables and fruits in their diet, rather than focusing on bread, cake, pizza, ice cream, and soda.

- Train and encourage them to cook nutritious meals on their own. Let them practice with you first. You may enjoy having family cooking time together! You may want to focus especially on simple, nutritious breakfasts and lunches.

- Teach and train them to be aware of their own medical needs. Help them understand their own limitations, without using medical issues as an excuse for not working. They need to understand the balance between working whenever they can, even though they may be a little under the weather, versus working when they should be home in bed. They should also feel comfortable with talking to others (for example, a doctor or other medical personnel) if they have medical questions, rather than waiting until a problem becomes serious.

Be truthful on the missionary application with emotional issues and explain any ongoing medical issues completely and fully. If your perspective missionary is on any regular medication for a physical condition, make sure that is explained on the missionary application as well.

SOCIAL PREPARATION

The use of social media has changed the way we communicate with each other. There are negative consequences to excessive use of such media. As a parent, you may want to monitor your future missionaries' use of electronics to make sure it is appropriate for one who is preparing to serve.

Here are some suggestions of ways you can help your child prepare socially for a mission:

- As a family, discuss in family home evening how the Internet, video games, television, smartphones, and movies are used in your home. Discuss how your family can control the use of media and entertainment better in your home. Come up with a plan as a family and think of ways to improve communication in the family. Even though social media is an effective way to share the gospel, social media should not be the sole means of communication with others. Texting during school classes and Church or while driving is inappropriate, and the negative consequences of such behavior should be discussed as a family.

- Limit video game playing to a couple of hours a week at most. Excessive gaming can easily become an addiction that is hard to break. When video games, TV, and movies are taken away (or severely restricted), missionaries can sometimes feel unable to cope with reality. This may also hinder a missionary's ability to be obedient!

- Have your future missionaries save money for their mission. Learning how to handle money wisely instills emotional strength, and social understanding, too. Missionaries will value their mission more and work harder if they have paid for (at least part of) the opportunity to serve. Involve them in family budgeting. As missionaries, they will be working with their companions in budgeting their monthly allowance. They will need to know how to live within this allowance and not go over budget. Help them to know how to live without any extras in their life and to distinguish between wants and needs. They will need to know how to do without when they do not have the money for something. Teach and practice having them pay their own tithing and fast offerings before anything else so that they will understand this principle through personal practice. This will also enable them to bear personal testimony to their investigators of the blessings that come from paying tithes and offerings.

- Teach them how to interact and talk with people of different age groups and backgrounds. Have them practice shaking hands with people and looking them in the eye when they speak to them. Have family home evening lessons on how to talk with people they do not know.

- Encourage them get a job, not only to earn money for their mission, but to let them have the experience of working and dealing with people under stressful circumstances.

- Invite people from different backgrounds and cultures into your home and encourage your children to be a part of the conversations that occur.

- If you live in locations with large LDS populations (such as Utah), go on family trips or travel to other places where they can interact with people from different backgrounds, ethnicities, religions, and even other countries if possible.

SPIRITUAL PREPARATION

For much of their spiritual preparation, you must lead out and set an example to your future missionaries with as many of these principles as possible. Regular temple attendance, priesthood interviews, prayer, scripture study, obedience, service, and having a firm testimony of the doctrine of Christ are all ways you can set that example.

Here are some suggestions:

- Help your future missionary to be worthy go to the temple and help young men to receive the priesthood. President Monson taught, "Young men, I admonish you to prepare for service as a missionary. Keep yourselves clean and pure and worthy to represent the Lord."[3] Parents, especially fathers, should be aware of the worthiness of their children. Elder M. Russell Ballard taught, "Fathers, not only do you have the right to know the worthiness of your children, you have the responsibility."[4]

- Prepare them now for the regular interviews they will have with their mission president by holding your own interviews with them. Follow the pattern of priesthood interviews—start and conclude with a prayer; help them feel comfortable; invite them to talk about what is really happening in their life and express their feelings; ask specific worthiness questions; bear testimony; and show love.

- Focus on daily prayer and study of the scriptures and *Preach My Gospel* individually and as a family. Prepare your future missionaries to be able to study the gospel for at least an hour each day individually, and for another hour with a companion. Have them gradually increase the amount of time they study each day as they approach the time of their call and subsequent departure. You may want to study Chapter 2 of *Preach My Gospel* for ideas on different ways to study more effectively. During family scripture study, share and discuss spiritual insights and feelings about verses of scripture.

- Teach and exemplify the principles of true obedience and of living the gospel. Obedience is the first law of heaven and of missionary work, too. Parents' examples say more than words.

Show them how to live the gospel through family service projects, magnifying callings, and sharing the gospel. Make sure that your words and actions exemplify support of and obedience to the counsel of local as well as general authorities.

- Teach and model the control and wise use of technology, entertainment, and social media. As a family, follow with exactness the Entertainment and Media standards in *For the Strength of Youth*. While social media and online proselyting are now a reality, control and moderation are still absolutely essential.

- Give them opportunities to teach and help them do so. Study and use the new Youth Curriculum in your home. Have them study and practice teaching the missionary lessons found in Chapter 3 of *Preach My Gospel* to your family.

- Teach them how to recognize and follow the promptings of the Holy Ghost and receive personal revelation. Study and apply Chapter 4 of *Preach My Gospel* in your family home evenings. Hold testimony meetings as a family regularly so your future missionaries can feel the Spirit as they testify of the truthfulness of the gospel of Jesus Christ.

Perhaps the most important spiritual preparation you can provide for your future missionaries is to help them understand and gain a strong testimony of the doctrine of Christ. This doctrine is the essence of the missionary purpose and of your eternal purpose as a family. Review Chapter 2 of this book with your family and discuss your eternal purpose. You may also want to read and study 2 Nephi 31, 3 Nephi 11, and 3 Nephi 27 together as a family. Discuss how these first principles or ordinances of the gospel continue to apply in our lives as we take the sacrament weekly and make temple covenants.

In this chapter, there have been many different suggestions to help prepare your children for missionary service. Please don't become overwhelmed, but pick two or three things that the Spirit whispers you should focus on. Then, make a plan as to how you will implement them into your home.

With the new lower ages for missionary service and the emphasis on hastening the work, there has never been a time when the church has needed "raised-bar" missionaries more than today. The success of raising the bar for missionary candidates depends on significantly increasing the help, support, teaching, and training done by parents. In other words, parents must raise their bar as well.

Elder M. Russell Ballard of the Quorum of the Twelve Apostles declared: "What we need now is the greatest generation of missionaries in the history of the Church. We need worthy, qualified, spiritually energized missionaries who, like Helaman's two thousand stripling warriors, are 'exceedingly valiant for courage, and also for strength and activity' and who are 'true at all times in whatsoever thing they [are] entrusted.'"[5] With your support, training, and leadership as their parents, future missionaries preparing to serve will be the best prepared, the most valiant, and the greatest generation of missionaries ever!

NOTES

1. Richard G. Scott, "Now Is the Time to Serve a Mission!" *Ensign, May* 2006.
2. David A .Bednar, "Becoming a Missionary," *Ensign,* November 2005.
3. Thomas S. Monson, "As We Meet Together Again," *Ensign*, November 2010.
4. M. Russell Ballard, "The Greatest Generation of Missionaries," *Ensign*, November 2002.
5. Ibid.

About the Authors

Marianna and Steve Richardson met and married while attending Brigham Young University (BYU). They love large families and have been abundantly blessed with twelve beautiful children. Seven of their children have married and they have twenty-three grandchildren (and counting). Eight of their children and six of their children-in-law have served full-time missions. They are looking forward to many more missionaries from their family in the future!

Both Marianna and Steve have master's degrees and doctorates. Marianna's graduate work is in education, focusing on special education, curriculum, and motivational research. She is currently an adjunct professor at the BYU Marriott School of Management. Steve's degrees are in linguistics and computer science. He worked for many years at both IBM and Microsoft Research and he currently manages the translation systems at the Church of Jesus Christ of Latter-day Saints. Both of them have authored several professional publications.

Marianna has served in many ward and stake auxiliary presidencies and is a consummate gospel doctrine teacher. Steve presided over the Brazil São Paulo South Mission from 2008 to 2011 and served previously as a bishop and stake president. Since returning from their service in Brazil, they have enjoyed teaching a weekly institute class for returned missionaries and giving monthly firesides to the parents of those missionaries.

Marianna spoke at BYU Education Week for two years before and after her mission with Steve. She published two previous books with

About the Authors

Cedar Fort: *C. S. Lewis: Latter-day Truths in Narnia* and *Alfred Edersheim: A Jewish Scholar for the Mormon Prophets*. In 2015, Steve and Marianna also lectured together at BYU Education Week on the topic of helping returned missionaries and their families.

Personal Notes

Personal Notes

Personal Notes

Personal Notes

Personal Notes

Personal Notes